D1736649

Managing the Design Process
Concept Development

ROCKPORT

© 2010 by Rockport Publishers, Inc.

All rights reserved. No part of this book may be reproduced
in any form without written permission of the copyright
owners. All images in this book have been reproduced with
the knowledge and prior consent of the artists concerned, and
no responsibility is accepted by producer, publisher, or printer
for any infringement of copyright or otherwise, arising from
the contents of this publication. Every effort has been made to
ensure that credits accurately comply with information supplied.
We apologize for any inaccuracies that may have occurred and
will resolve inaccurate or missing information in a subsequent
reprinting of the book.

First published in the United States of America by
Rockport Publishers, a member of
Quayside Publishing Group
100 Cummings Center
Suite 406-L
Beverly, Massachusetts 01915-6101
Telephone: (978) 282-9590
Fax: (978) 283-2742
www.rockpub.com

Library of Congress Cataloging-in-Publication Data
Stone, Terry Lee.
  Managing the design process--concept development : an
essential manual for the working designer / Terry Lee Stone.
      p. cm.
  Includes bibliographical references and index.
  ISBN-13: 978-1-59253-617-7
  ISBN-10: 1-59253-617-4
  1. Commercial art--Management. 2. Design services--
Management. 3. Creation (Literary, artistic, etc.) I. Title. II. Title:
Essential manual for the working designer.
  NC1001.S76 2010
  741.6068--dc22

                                        2010001782
                                        CIP

ISBN-13: 978-1-59253-617-7
ISBN-10: 1-59253-617-4

10 9 8 7 6 5 4 3 2 1

Design: AdamsMorioka, Inc.

Printed in China

Managing the Design Process
Concept Development
An Essential Manual for the Working Designer

Terry Lee Stone

BEVERLY MASSACHUSETTS

ROCKPORT PUBLISHERS

Contents

Introduction   6–9
How to Use This Book
Managing the Design Process

The Design Process   10–11

Chapter 1: Applied Creativity   12–25
Creativity in a Business Environment
Defining Design's Power Role
How Designers Work
Choosing a Designer
Five ways to Determine a Good Designer–Client Match

Chapter 2: Big Goals   26–57
Design in an Ever-Changing World
Design Thinking
Design Supports Internal Communications
Socially Responsible Design
Measuring Design
Making the Most of Design Investment

Chapter 3: Design-Centric Research   58–77
The Importance of Research for Design
Research Aligns and Focuses Design
Design Research is About Better Design Thinking
Three Useful Research Tactics
Defining the Audience: Demographics and Ethnography
Defining the Audience: Psychographics
Defining the Medium

Chapter 4: Strategic Thinking 78–111

Design and Strategy

What is Design Strategy?

Design as a Business Tool

Developing a Design Strategy

Managing Aesthetic Strategy

Evaluating Design Strategy

Articulating Design Strategy

Common Mistakes in Design Strategy

Chapter 5: Informed Risk Taking 112–131

Taking Creative Risks

Assessing Risk

Risk versus Uncertainty

Building Courage

Innovative Design Means Taking a Calculated Risk

Presenting Risky Ideas

Chapter 6: Creative Briefs 132–151

Creative Briefs are Strategic Tools

How to do a Creative Brief

The 10 Most Important Things to Include in a Creative Brief

Managing to a Creative Brief

What's Included in a Design Criteria?

Who Uses a Creative Brief?

Going Without a Creative Brief

Chapter 7: Aesthetic Considerations 152–187

Aesthetic in Design

Well-Designed Goes Beyond Pretty

Aesthetic Components

Mapping Aesthetics

Understanding Aesthetic Dynamics in Design

Evaluating Aesthetic Choices

How to Do a Design Critique

Betting Aesthetic Ideas Approved

Chapter 8: Managing Expectations 188–199

How to Manage Client Expectations

Four Best Practices for Successfully Managing Client Expectations

Communication and Design Management

Ongoing Design Management

Directory of Contributors 200–201

Index 202–205

Bibliography and Resources 206–207

Acknowledgments 208

About the Author 208

Introduction

Every aspect of business is impacted by design—from the products or services a company provides, to the various forms of communications that express these products and services, to the many environments, physical or virtual, where customers interact with these offerings. Graphic design can captivate, persuade, motivate, and delight. Because of this, graphic design's enormous power to connect a business on an emotional level with its customers is unparalleled. Happily, this power is becoming acknowledged not just by designers but also by the majority of their clients as well.

It seems that businesses and organizations of all types are starting to understand that good design can give a product a distinct competitive advantage over other products in the same category, which will inevitably benefit their company's bottom line. What is not clear to many is the intricate collaborative partnership between designer and client that is required to not only achieve a great design but also to utilize it to its full capacity through a series of strategic steps. *Managing the Design Process* is precisely about that collaboration.

This book is about how to harness the power of graphic design in a real and practical manner. To understand how this collaborative process works will require learning some new language, as well as tools and techniques, in the application of design management and its associated concept design leadership. Because this is such an emerging discourse, there is not yet complete agreement in the design industry on exactly how to define these very different, but related, activities. In fact, for some designers, these terms are interchangeable. For the purpose of this book, here is a working definition of each term:

Design Management
The process of coordinating and directing design resources to achieve a stated objective

Design Leadership
The process of utilizing design as a management tool to determine and achieve strategic goals

With these definitions, design management has more of a tactical focus, while design leadership is more visionary. Design leadership is about

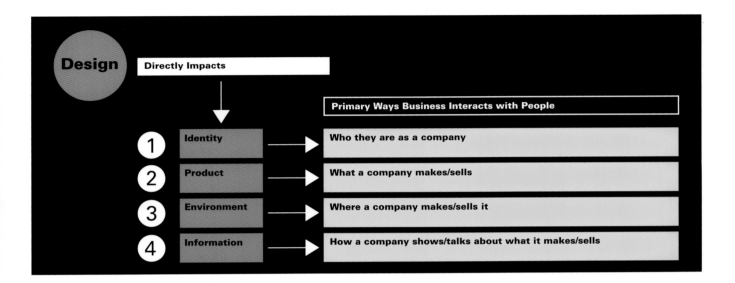

Design | **Directly Impacts**

Primary Ways Business Interacts with People

1 **Identity** → Who they are as a company

2 **Product** → What a company makes/sells

3 **Environment** → Where a company makes/sells it

4 **Information** → How a company shows/talks about what it makes/sells

framing a design problem, the solution of which will move forward a client's business goals. This means acquiring input and research, analyzing and processing this information, and then developing a strategy or conceptual solution. Design management, defined this way, concerns itself with utilizing the people and procedures required to actually make a design solution happen. Design leadership requires creative courage and non-traditional thinking. Design management needs methodical planning and meticulous practice.

Every graphic design project needs both activities employed at different stages of the design development cycle. This book will be primarily focused on managing and leading the development of ideas, concepts, and plans. The second volume of the *Managing the Design Process* series will focus more on design management of processes, people, and implementation. Both books will feature practical, not theoretical, stories, trade secrets, and successful methodologies from real designers and their clients.

Traits of Managers versus Leaders

Warren Bennis, the American scholar, author, and organizational expert who is regarded as a pioneer in leadership studies, defined a clear dichotomy in the behavior of managers and leaders. He observed the following twelve distinctions between the two groups:

Managers administer	Leaders innovate
Managers ask how and when	Leaders ask what and why
Managers focus on systems	Leaders focus on people
Managers do things right	Leaders do the right things
Managers maintain	Leaders develop
Managers rely on control	Leaders inspire trust
Managers have short-term perspective	Leaders have long-term perspective
Managers accept the status quo	Leaders challenge the status quo
Managers have an eye on the bottom line	Leaders have an eye on the horizon
Managers imitate	Leaders originate
Managers emulate the classic good soldier	Leaders are their own person
Managers copy	Leaders show originality

How to Use This Book

What this book offers is a behind-the-scenes look at what it actually takes to get great design concepts approved. The designers featured in this book are willing to let us in on what design management and leadership means in their work. Beyond aesthetics, they share both the intellectual and emotional aspects of their client collaborations. Breaking down their project development procedures, they let us examine creative decision making, along with the inevitable compromises, required for great design.

Some key things to observe and take away from the case studies and project profiles presented in this book that can help you in your practice:

▶ What kind of research is done on the project and how extensive is it? What did they learn and was it worth the effort?

▶ How did the designer translate this discovery information into a design concept? Would you have made a similar creative choice?

▶ What tools did the designer use to help convince their client that the concept was right? Could you adapt these tools for use with your clients?

▶ What issues or concerns did the client have about the design? How were these addressed? What kind of risk was required on the part of the client to accept the designer's recommendations?

▶ How were the designs evaluated and tested? What insights were gained and how did that affect further design refinements?

▶ After all was said and done, what is the finished design? What delivery medium was used? Was it effective? What do you personally think of it?

Managing the Design Process

Graphic designers have a series of repeatable steps and procedures that make them true professionals. In each client relationship, they follow the same systematic phases of work that allows them to consistently produce a result. Different designers may have different terms for these steps, but all of them employ something similar. On the following pages you will find the design process chart illustrating this systematic project work flow.

This chart provides an overview of how a design goes from concept to completion. It is a model that can be modified to suit any design project. It serves as an outline of the interactions between designer and client as work progresses.

Things that most affect the phases of work diagrammed in the design process chart:

Communication:
Timely and effective communication and knowledge sharing throughout the process is necessary. Incomplete or lax communication will sabotage design.

Scope Of Work:
Massive projects may require repetition of certain phases, while smaller projects with less complexity may combine steps.

Timing:
Compressed schedules mean shortening phases and skipping details. Luxurious timeframes allow for more extensive work in each phase.

Budget:
Less money equals less work. Large budgets accommodate more work through more lengthy and involved procedures.

Delivery Media:
Choice of delivery medium can mean more (or less) extensive collaboration with other types of collaborators and can affect the process.

Design management means doing everything possible to manage and support a designer's ability to achieve favorable outcomes in each phase of developing design.

The Design Process

Discover

1 Project Initiation

- Client identifies need or goal
- Client develops preliminary budget
- Client develops preliminary schedule
- If possible, client creates preliminary creative brief
- Client identifies potential designers and contacts them
- Client and designer meet for preliminary discussion and portfolio review
- Client creates and sends out RFP (request for proposals)
- Designers respond and submit proposal for design services
- Client accepts proposal and confirms designer
- Designer typically requests deposit payment on the project

Goal of this phase:
- Establish Basic Project Parameters
- Selection of Designer

2 Orientation/ Research

- Client provides any relevant background information and materials
- Designer leads client through creative briefing sessions
- Client and designer commence research as needed regarding
  Competitive landscape
  Target audience
  Market research
  Design research
  Using any or all of the following:
  Observation
  Interviews
  Questionnaires
  Audits
- Client and designer confirm any technical or functionality parameters
- Client and designer confirm needs assessment and begin design problem formulation

Goal of this phase:
- Clarify Objectives and Goals
- Identify Opportunities
- Set Broad-based Requirements

Define

3 Strategy

- Designer analyzes and synthesizes the research and information gathered
- Designer develops design criteria
- Designer develops functionality criteria
- Designer develops media delivery method plan
- Designer presents all of the above for client input or approval
- Designer develops and articulates a strategy for the design
- Designer develops preliminary plans: information architecture, pagination maps, and/or wireframes (if appropriate)
- Designer presents all of the above for client input or approval

Goal of this phase:
- Overall Strategy
- Design Approach
- Confirmed List of Deliverables

4 Exploration

- Based on client-approved strategy, designer develops preliminary design concepts
- Designer's ideation can take the following forms
  Roughs/thumbnails/ sketches
  Storyboards
  Flowcharts
  Mood/theme boards
  Look and feel
  POP (Proof of Principal) or Proof of Concept Models
- Designer presents the above to client for discussion, input, and approval
- Client provides insights and initial validation that the concept direction will meet the project's stated goals and objectives
- Typically, the designer will create several alternative concepts that will be narrowed down to only a couple of concept ideas to be developed further.

Goal of this phase:
- Generate Preliminary Ideas
- Evaluate these Ideas

← Understand → ◄► Ideate

Develop

Deliver

| **5** | **6** | **7** | **8** | **9** |

Development
Refinement
Production
Manufacture/ Launch
Project Completion

---

5 — Development

- Based on client-approved concept ideas, designer further develops the design concept(s).
- These further iterations of the concept(s) will be provided as tighter representations of the design:
  Comprehensive layouts
  Animatics
  Typical pages or spreads
  Preliminary Prototypes
- These will incorporate preliminary, often placeholder
  Copy/Messaging
  Imagery
  Motion
  Audio
- Designer presents the above to client for discussion, input, and approval
- Client provides insights and validation that the design direction will meet the project's stated goals and objectives
- Typically, the client will approve one design direction that will then be refined by the designer

6 — Refinement

- With a client-approved design direction, designer further refines the design.
- Typically, the changes/ modifications are
  Based specifically on client requests
  Minor in nature
  Finessing of aesthetic elements
- Designer presents the above to client for discussion, input, and approval
- Testing of the design may occur, and this may lead to another round of refinements. Testing may include:
  Validation
  Usability testing
  Designer would then present these additional refinements to client for approval
- Designer initiates preproduction meeting with additional team members, if needed. These might include:
  Printer, Fabricator, Manufacturer, Photographer, Illustrator, Audio engineer, Programmer

7 — Production

- With an approved design, the designer begins implementation of the design across all the required deliverables. This may include:
  Print: *mechanicals/key lines, finished art, digital files, camera ready art, all elements final*
  Web: *modeling phase, detailed flowchart, all content, finished art for pages and graphic elements, programming, testing*
  Motion: *creating all project elements, animation making movies, shooting live action, editing, final rendering, mastering*
  Environment: *specifications, final prototyping, 3-D digital models, testing in preparation for production, coordinate/manage technical team*
  Packaging: *high-resolution file prep per specifications, color correction, structural prototyping*

8 — Manufacture/Launch

- Depending on the project and delivery media, the production materials are often handed over by the designer to others. Although other professionals outside the design firm actually do the work in most instances, the designer must supervise these suppliers and their work. This can include:
  Pre-Press/Separator/ Printer
  Fabricator/Manufacturer
  Engineer/Programmer
  Media outlet
  Broadcast/on-air
  Launched on Web/live
- Designer may be engaged in the supervision or management of any or all of the above suppliers or it may be the client's responsibility
- Ongoing maintenance, especially in the case of Web design, may be an aspect of the project, or it will be determined under a separate agreement

9 — Project Completion

- Designer and client have a project debriefing (exit interview) to review
  Project procedures
  Outcomes: success or failure
  Feedback loops
  Additional opportunities
- Designer archives project files. Also, writes up a case study while the project details are fresh. This is preparation for the project as a self-promotional tool.
- Designer closes out and invoices project
- Client pays designer

Goal of this phase:
- Further Develop Ideas
- Select a Design Direction

Goal of this phase:
- Final Design Approved

Goal of this phase:
- Final Production
- Materials for Release

Goal of this phase:
- Design Materials
- Completed and in Use

Goal of this phase:
- Relationship building
- Sales opportunity for designer
- Begin new project

Execute

Chapter 1
Applied Creativity

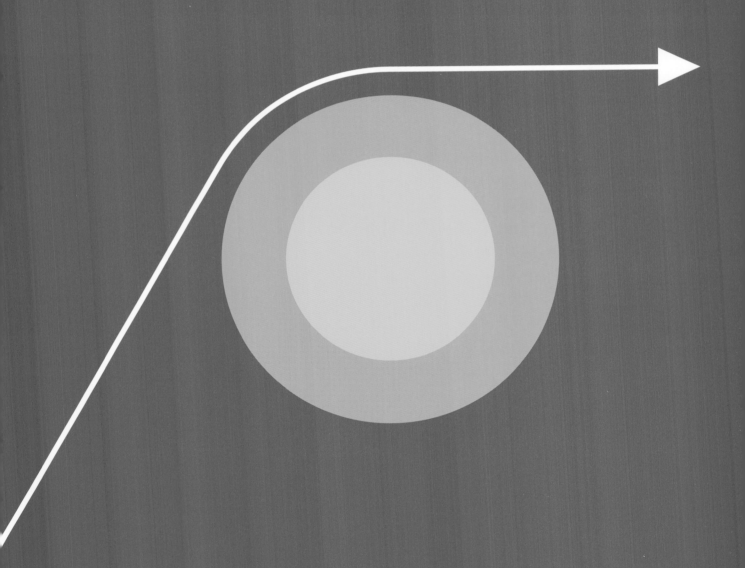

Creativity in a Business Environment

Design is a process, a service, a way of thinking, and an activity that results in objects, systems, artifacts, and outcomes. These results must all work aesthetically, functionally, and commercially. In short, design is applied creativity.

Design is not just for designers. At the very least, it involves a client—someone with a problem, goal, or objective—who engages the designer to provide solutions or meet needs. Design can serve a person, company, product, service, or idea. The client usually has someone they are directing these efforts toward—a customer, community, or audience, and it is typically commissioned by one person, but intended for another. According to AIGA, the professional association for design, "The act of designing is an inherently powerful act. In that act, we share the stage with CEOs, government officials, civic leaders, passionate activists, and fellow citizens." Getting a handle on the collaborative nature of design required to deal with all these variable factors is no small task.

The Design Council UK says, "Good design is a quantifiable benefit, not a cost. Its value can be measured economically, socially, and environmentally." Design is a balance of many factors, some objective and some subjective. Clients' business or organization requirements, technical parameters, cost and time constraints, are all measurable and objective things. While aesthetic preferences, interpretations of design elements like color and form, emotional reactions, and cultural influences are all subjective.

Everything manmade is designed by someone, so it makes sense to consider exactly how and why things are designed. Every business' requires a designed identity, environment, business papers, sales and marketing materials, and a website. It's inevitable. Recognizing this and investing in a great design, rather than letting it just happen, is a key ingredient in every successful business.

More and more, clients recognize the value of design. But not every client really understands how to work with a designer. Getting the best out of their design consultants, participating in the process, and effectively interacting with creative people takes practice. Some clients do it over and over. There are individuals who are tasked with this job in large organizations. Small business owners may hire a designer once and rarely after that, simply maintaining the design they started with.

Many designers have trouble managing the design process on their end as well. They have trouble planning and implementing. There are myriad details to deal with, and lots of personalities—from clients to design team to outside suppliers. When you boil it all down, the actual creative act of ideation, is about thirty percent of the project, with seventy percent of the time dealing with issues of facilitation, communication, technology, relationships, expectations, technical specifications, manufacturing, etc. In short, any given job will be largely dealing with management of the design process.

Project Profile in Applied Creativity
HGM Branding designed by Alt Group / Auckland, New Zealand

Hudson Gavin Martin (HGM) is a boutique legal practice formed by three partners, who advise on intellectual property and technology law in Australia. Multidisciplinary design studio, Alt Group, based in Auckland, New Zealand, worked to develop a visual identity, environment, and range of communication tools that challenged expectations of how legal service firms express their brand. "The experience was conceived of as an ongoing conversation that reveals 'ideas' that come in threes," explains Alt managing director, Ben Corban. "Three is more than a partnership—it's a team. Culture and customs offer up all sorts of threesomes, humorous and otherwise."

RIGHT
The identity uses the copyright, trademark, and registered symbols to directly reference the firm's core business. The registered symbol couldn't be legally used until the logotype was registered with IPONZ (Intellectual Property Office of NZ). An interim "'launch" logotype was produced with an asterisk and small copy (Registration Pending) in place of the ® symbol until registration was complete.

BELOW
Copy became a key part of the identity to assist in communicating the company culture and offering. "The three wise men, Hudson, Gavin, Martin, are cool, calm, and collected. They advise on clients' equities, assets, and liabilities and are ready, willing, and able," says Alt creative director Dean Poole. "A three-word copy approach was used across a range of collateral—for example, in the brochure above, the three-word groupings run into each other like concrete poetry."

The company name is revealed in clean typographic signage, (below, top). The brand idea of three related words that symbolize Hudson Gavin Martin was extended to the environment through corporate art and environmental graphics as well. A custom carpet signals a welcome, with the words: Hop, Skip, and Jump. Text-based and image-only artworks reveal the trilogy of business—like the knife, fork, and spoon posters, (below).

A hat trick placed on a triangle-shaped plinth, made from three bowler hats and a bronze apple, (above), continues the symbolic reference to the three-way partnership. In the boardroom hangs a modernist triptych constructed from red, green, and blue LEGO bricks. Framed posters, like Bacon Lettuce Tomato, (below, bottom), echo the three-word idea as well as picnics with a bright-red, checked background that suggests a tablecloth.

Core elements of the Hudson Gavin Martin identity and the tools of the intellectual property trade—the ©, ® and ™ symbols were incorporated to spell out the word *Christmas*. "The concept of three is an important part of the Hudson Gavin Martin brand," notes Alt creative director, Dean Poole. "Christmas was stated three times and the gift itself was in three parts—wine, a rolling pin, and a candle—all the ingredients for a celebration or three. A holy trinity, if you will."

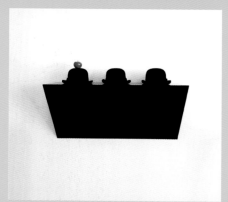

BELOW
The copy strategy of three key words was extended into the website page headers—Hello, Hello, Hello; Signed, Sealed, Delivered; Shake, Rattle, Roll; Extra, Extra, Extra. The Hudson Gavin Martin site was built on a bespoke content-management platform to allow self-publishing of relevant issues based articles and campaign elements for recruitment and promotion.

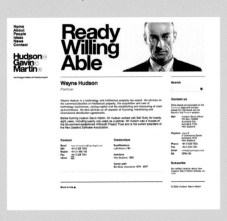

Design's Importance to Clients

The Danish Design Centre (DDC) has developed the concept of a design "ladder" that describes four levels of commitment to design that clients may have:

Step One: Nondesign

Design is inconspicuous and performed by staff members who are not design professionals. Design solutions are created based on "shared perceptions of functionality and aesthetics." End-users needs and points of view are not considered.

Step Two: Design Is Styling

Design is viewed as the final aesthetic finish only. Sometimes it is created by designers, but generally, other professionals are involved.

Step Three: Design as Process

Design is viewed as a work method and adopted early. Design solutions are focused on end-user requirements. Design is seen as a multidisciplinary approach that requires a variety of expertise.

Step Four: Design as Innovation

The designer collaborates with client executives in adopting an innovative approach to substantial parts of their business. The design processes are combined with the company vision to impact al aspects of the client's products or services.

Defining Design's Power Role

Everything, but especially communication, is becoming increasingly complex. Things change so rapidly due to technology and new ways of interacting as human beings. It had given us more connectivity, but in many ways, less time to enjoy it. Plus product life cycles are shorter, and there is increased competition and a much higher demand for productivity and quality. There is also simply so much competition for everyone's limited attention. We may have become multitaskers, but you have to wonder how well any of us is accomplishing the task at hand. With increased capabilities there are also increased expectations; therefore, there's no feeling of ever really "advancing."

The power of design is that it helps us to rise above these conditions and gets people connected with products and services in real and meaningful ways. Some things clients can expect design to help them accomplish:

- Establish or improve an image
- Identify them (clearly show who/what they are)
- Articulate the brand, its mission, and promises
- Differentiate them, make a product or service stand out from competitors
- Alleviate uncertainty and confusion in the marketplace
- Understand and track performance against competitors

- Boost aesthetic appeal
- Cut through overwhelming amounts of information
- Properly position the product or service
- Develop targeted message
- Package a product or service
- Communicate the benefits and advantages of a product or service

- Establish or improve customer connections/relationships
- Help develop new markets, audiences, customers
- Delight the audience
- Create emotional resonance
- Produce memorable experiences
- Inspire loyalty, commitment, and investment

- Connect with employees and stakeholders
- Aid in recruitment
- Reduce costs or improve ROI
- Increase sales and profits
- Harness technology to support goals
- Provide value to clients and their customers

- Be sustainable, responsible corporate citizens
- Create or enhance symbolic or perceptual values
- Create language and meaning
- Capture cultural trends, and tap into and shape the zeitgeist

Project Profile in Applied Creativity
Benjamin Bixby Identity designed by Iconologic and André Benjamin / Atlanta, Georgia USA

Brand design firm Iconologic worked closely with musician/actor/entrepreneur André Benjamin, a.k.a. André 3000, to develop the identity for his Benjamin Bixby menswear collection brand—its platform, name, and identity system. The balloon is found on most of the clothing. The team's work mirrors the strong design point of view seen in the garments, one that both embraces and challenges tradition, and is meant to appeal to those with a distinct sense of adventure. This approach is evident in all of the sales and marketing materials as well.

BELOW
"Our clients understand that the story they tell, the experience they become, and the image they embody must be designed with the same likeness and risk as the product they create," says Iconologic creative director, Matt Rollins. "Risk is crucial to the process, and fearlessness brings great rewards."

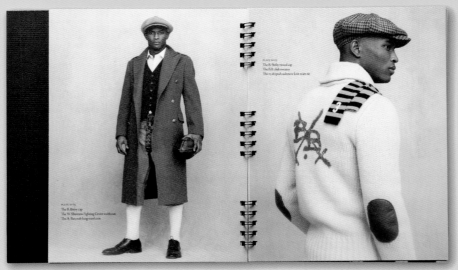

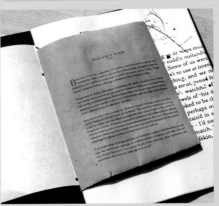

How Designers Work

Every designer is both an artist and a businessperson. That duality exists in every aspect of their work and practice—whether in their own studio, or their work for a design firm, or their work as part of an in-house design team. They must be creative on demand one moment and professional the next. They might be in artist mode playing around with colors, shapes, type, and imagery, and be interrupted to take a phone call, or an email, requiring them to discuss the details of client deliverables, budget adjustments, or technical specifications for a manufacturing processes. Design is a constant juggling of both art and commerce. It's what keeps the sometimes antagonistic nature of designing so interesting to so many people.

Whether they have on their business hat or art hat, designers are interested in ideas. Generating concept-based innovations across a range of delivery media in a variety of forms is how they spend their days. Sometimes, a design assignment is about novelty—creating something distinct and different. Other projects call for a unique spin to an existing or well-regarded approach—evolving the tried and true. Either way, the designer is asked to review, analyze, and ideate about the situation at hand.

Looking at the creative aspect of design reveals it to be an iterative process. One glance at the design process chart on pages 10–11 gives you an understanding of the scope of the many steps required. However, when looking at only the idea development phases (5 and 6 on the process chart), we see that the designer is constantly working with a diverse tangent of ideas. Hopefully, these various ideas come together in a cohesive way to form a design concept that satisfies the client. Sometimes, it means looping back and redoing certain steps in each phase to get to great design solutions.

Design Idea Flow

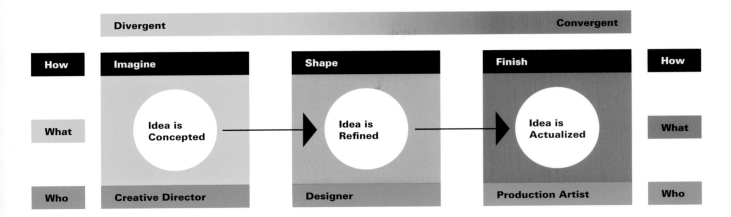

Flow of Design Ideas

As the design moves through the process toward completion, it is much more contained, logical, and apparent, which is why you'll often find the visionary creative director establishing the look and feel and central concept—an imaginative solution—that gets presented to a client and is approved in theory. The design concept is then passed along to a senior designer. They incorporate changes as well as client or creative director feedback, to refine, shape, and further develop the design. It gets presented again, and is approved by the client. The design then moves on to a junior designer or production artist who actually implements it.

Collaborative or Solo Workflow

The traditional workflow of a design is to start with the highly creative expert and end with the highly technical one. Experience and skill levels vary, but so does specific design expertise. Those who come up with great ideas can't always execute them. Different skills are required as the process progresses from rough idea to finished object. A designer should explain this to her clients. Doing so will alleviate the notion that the client is going from senior to junior staff member because the project is less interesting or requires less of the senior person's time. The truth is, the

client is better served as the project is handed to the next design team member with the most expertise in that phase of work. This disaggregating of the design tasks allows the best possible person to be focusing their talent on a particular aspect.

In the case of a solo designer with no additional team members, the designer must handle all aspects of the work. This requires them to be well rounded and good at all the tasks involved. Philosophically, some designers believe in one person handling a project from start to finish. The rationale being that this person is the most knowledgeable about the client and the project, although necessarily the specific task. They service the project based on a solid understanding of the design concept.

Clients should be made aware of which workflow and service model their designer is using. Both methodologies have their advantages and disadvantages. Mostly, it is a case of the scale of the design firm, the project, and the client. When establishing a new client relationship, the designer/design team should clearly explain how they work and who the client will be working with specifically in each phase of the project.

Design Team Flow

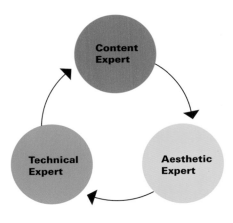

Project Profile in Applied Creativity

Times of India, Ganesha Campaign designed by Umbrella Design / Mumbai, India

The Times of India

Umbrella Design is one of few specialty design houses in India. Based in Mumbai (Bombay), the firm is lead by managing director Bhupal Rhamnathkar, executive creative director Deven Sansare, and chief operating officer Farhad F. Elavia. Umbrella Design has worked with the English-language daily newspaper, *The Times of India*, on their annual Ganesha festival ad campaign.

The campaign is bilingual, with one subject in English and three in Marathi, the state language, and tries to capture the spirit of the festival as it is celebrated by the people. "Since a new and relevant category, 'Most Eco-friendly Decoration' was added to the contest this year," notes Rhamnathkar, "the focus of the campaign is the new category. We've also created a special graphic unit to highlight the new category."

BELOW LEFT AND OPPOSITE
"At the beginning of the twentieth century, Indian nationalist and social reformer Bal Gangadhar Tilak decided to take Ganesha out of the house and into the street to celebrate the Hindu deity's festival in public," explains Umbrella Design executive creative director Deven Sansare. "Tilak's agenda was to unite people under a common cause that would not be seen by the British colonial administration as political. Today, the practice continues and various organizations organize and celebrate 'public' Ganesha festivals."

BELOW
It is a common practice in India to "see" and "find" the distinctive elephant form of Hindu god Ganesha in the most unlikely of objects. Taking that as the starting point, Umbrella Design developed the ecofriendly logo using the three-arrow recycle symbol, but also made it reminiscent of aspects of an elephant's curving form.

Ways to Determine a Good Designer–Client Match

The following tips are key indicators for both clients and designers to use to determine compatibility and competence:

1

Background:
Research them. Do your homework and visit their website. Who are they? What do they make? How do they present themselves?

2

Expertise:
Is the designer's previous experience relevant to the project at hand? What kind of projects is the designer capable of handling? Are they a problem solver? Regarding clients, how much control do they need/want over the design process?

3

Professionalism:
How do they conduct themselves? Do they have references? What is their attitude? Do they have good communication skills? Are they well connected to supplementary team members or experts required on the project?

4

Chemistry:
Do you like this person? Would you have a meal with them? Who exactly will be working on this project?

5

Parameters:
Does the time frame and budget work? Can you come to basic terms? Will this project be a priority or one of many?

Choosing a Designer

If you are a graphic designer, then you know all too well that one of the hard, yet fascinating, things about design is that it requires so many kinds of knowledge and thought—from conceptual through technical. If you are a client, it can be very difficult to discern one designer's expertise over another's. Think about how hard it is for them to choose the right design consultant when all the designers they meet seem to use the same language in explaining the advantages of hiring one firm over another. Plus few designers speak of their expertise in terms of a strategic business investment with measurable results.

Because of this conflict and confusion, you can see how choosing a designer often becomes simply a beauty contest. Which designer has the body of work that appeals to the client the most? Or perhaps, the selection is based on the designer's client roster; which designer has the most dazzling client list? Or maybe it all comes down to money; whose bid meets the client's budget?

So many clients fail to conduct a hiring interview for a designer in a way that helps them discern who has the best track record on problems like theirs. Relevant experience with another kind of client may not result in creating designs that this new client likes or even recognizes the value of. Clients also often fail to figure out who is a good fit temperamentally for their organization. It's hard to know which designer will do the best job. For these reasons, designers must become able to articulate their contributions toward meeting a client's needs, rather than dwell on discussions of aesthetics alone.

Project Profile in Applied Creativity
Leccia Catalog designed by Change Is Good / Paris, France

Contemporary French painter/photographer/ filmmaker Ange Leccia is a lecturer at the Ecole des Beaux-Arts de Cergy-Pontoise. He also heads a research unit for young artists, called Le Pavillon, at the Palais de Tokyo, a museum dedicated to modern and contemporary art. He works primarily in photography and video. For Leccia's video art installation at the Museum Bourdelle, the Paris-based design duo of José Albergaria and Rik Bas Backer, known as Change Is Good, created a catalog that reveals the artist's work using full-size images in spreads without interruption, like a film. "This is a book that obliges the reader to see Ange Leccia's video images first. For this, we left the book sheets uncut in order to have a book only with these dark mysterious images, a solution to give more depth to the work," explains Albergaria. In order to fully view the catalog, the reader must slit open the pages—a very intriguing bindery solution. Once the pages are slit open, the book will never look the same again.

BELOW
The catalog for the art exhibition features video-captured images from the films of Ange Leccia, ten projects of Le Pavillon students, and the font URW Grotesk designed by Professor Hermann Zapf. The catalog's pages actively engage the reader, and focus their attention on Leccia's mysterious imagery.

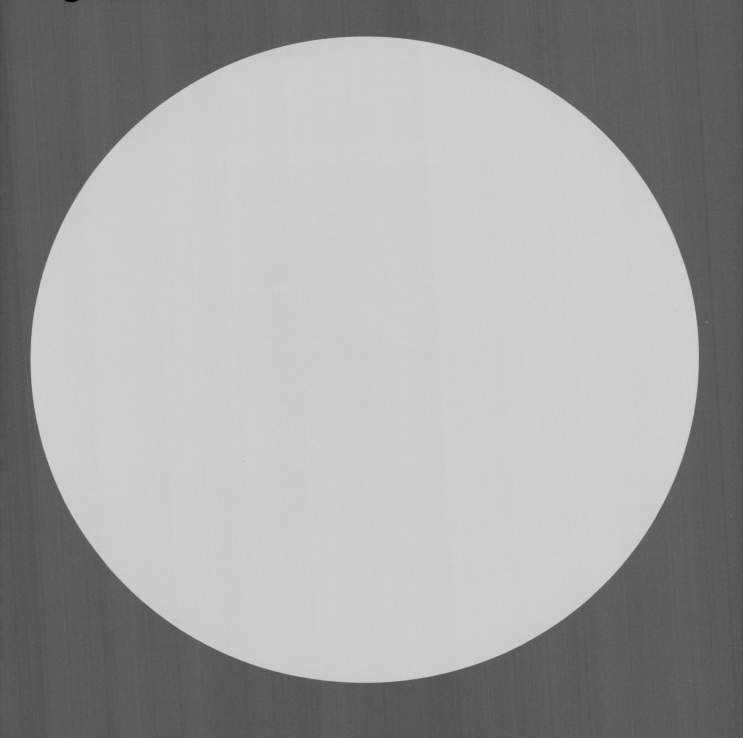

Design in an Ever-Changing World

Graphic design can't cure cancer. It could, however, bring attention to the cause, solicit funding and investment, facilitate community discussions, celebrate success stories, and help make dealing with it a bit easier. Design can play a number of different and valuable roles in supporting any organization's or business's big goals. These tend to be goals that go beyond a client's bottom line.

Design helps audiences participate in a better future, or it can support a purely commercial purpose. Good design can motivate action in either case. A few years back, there was a so-called "designism" movement—the idea that design could save the world, especially through political activism. In the ensuing years, the movement didn't gather a lot of consolidated or coordinated efforts. The idea of designers using their powers for good has become a much more personal pursuit, with each designer following his or her own conscience. With the shrinking nature of global society, brought about by technologically enabled community connections and driven by the world's decreasing resources, designers collectively will be called upon to play their part in solving the world's problems. Mostly, this will happen through well-considered work for their clients. Maybe design can't change the world, but just maybe, design thinking can help.

Design Helps Meet Goals

How design is leveraged and managed across a variety of complex and global issues is an exciting thing to be involved in. Doing this effectively calls upon all of a designer's skills and knowledge base. Getting a big problem to solve and rising to the occasion makes for an exhilarating design project. It is especially satisfying if the design supports a product or category where end-users have low expectations for clarity, functionality, or visual appeal. Swooping in and providing great design in that context accelerates the client's goals—commercial or altruistic, and cements customer loyalty.

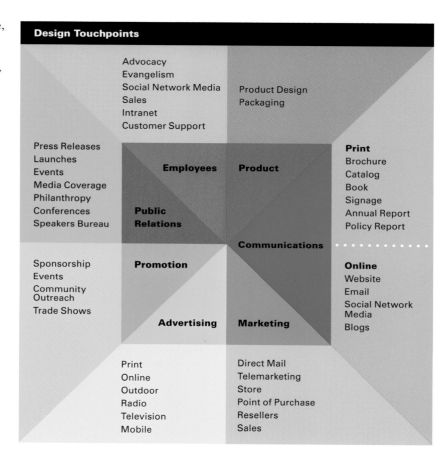

Design Touchpoints

Advocacy
Evangelism
Social Network Media
Sales
Intranet
Customer Support

Product Design
Packaging

Press Releases
Launches
Events
Media Coverage
Philanthropy
Conferences
Speakers Bureau

Employees

Product

Public Relations

Print
Brochure
Catalog
Book
Signage
Annual Report
Policy Report

Communications

Sponsorship
Events
Community Outreach
Trade Shows

Promotion

Online
Website
Email
Social Network Media
Blogs

Advertising

Marketing

Print
Online
Outdoor
Radio
Television
Mobile

Direct Mail
Telemarketing
Store
Point of Purchase
Resellers
Sales

Some of the many design touchpoints that can be utilized to deliver great design to an audience in a way that helps clients meet their big goals.

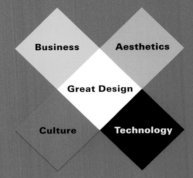

ABOVE
Great design is at the nexus of several sometimes competing factors, primarily business, aesthetics, culture, and technology. Finding a balanced response for each project is at the heart of increasing design's potential for meeting goals.

Design in this sense works with brand equity—the reputation and powerful feelings consumers have about a product or service—to amplify trust, the bottom line, and makes society a better place for all of us. On a practical level, it gets consumers to try new things or buy more of the existing ones. So design applied consistently across all the places where a consumer interacts with a client's brand—the design touchpoints—creates immediate recognition, comfort, and allegiance. This allows a client to be bold and deliver their message in a way that consumers are most receptive.

Shifting Values

As our society's values shift away from mass consumption to more individual or carefully considered buying behaviors, sustainability and social responsibility become significant factors in what is perceived as quality—no matter what the clients' product or service is. These ideas will definitely impact design. Many designers are rethinking their roles and counseling their clients to make sure that their work together is both necessary and responsible. Going forward, designers will be called upon to use all their skills to solve immediate and long-term problems.

Although it is not likely that designers will turn down business, citing altruism over healthy self interest (i.e., making a living), it is likely that the nature of graphic design practice will evolve with the times as it always has. Primarily driven by technological changes, but increasingly to be impacted by cultural value shifts and the demand for environmentally correct solutions.

Designers now, and always will, ask the tough questions of their clients. The case studies in this chapter focus on how design thinking was employed to meet several of the major goals facing so many clients, including: innovation, globalization, employee communications, sustainability, and the branding of experience.

Design Thinking

Design thinking is a popular buzzword in the product or industrial design profession. But what does it mean? Victor Lombardi, visiting professor at Pratt Institute, one of the leading U.S. design schools, has defined "Design Thinking." Here's a synopsis:

- **Collaborative:**
  Working with others who have different and complementary skills to form agreement and generate better work.
- **Abductive:**
  Inventing new and better options to solve problems.
- **Experimental:**
  Posing hypotheses, building prototypes, and testing them in an iterative process.
- **Personal:**
  Considering each unique context and set of people in any given problem.
- **Integrative:**
  Perceiving and creating an entire system.
- **Interpretive:**
  Devising how to frame an issue or problem, then judging the possible solutions against this.

Case Study in Big Goals: Innovation

Chase Design Group / Los Angeles, California USA

Chase Design Group, lead by creative director Margo Chase, believes that questions can liberate great ideas from the chains of assumption. The firm challenges themselves and their clients to embrace the "why?" and the "what if?" This is a group of designers that knows that award-winning design doesn't happen by accident. They believe it's the product of many minds working together, and it starts with open-ended questions. It is a philosophical stance that fosters innovation. By working to push their thinking higher and their designs farther, Chase Design Group helps their clients to achieve unexpected results and engage their audiences in entirely new ways.

CVS/pharmacy: Beauty 360

CVS/pharmacy decided to make prestige beauty retailing accessible by launching a new chain of stores. Chase was enlisted to bring this retail vision to life. To understand the competition, an audit of primary competitors, like Sephora, Ulta, and Boots were studied. The strengths and weaknesses of each competitor were reviewed in depth to better understand what makes these companies successful. Following this research, Chase engaged in a naming exercise with CVS and their customers, resulting in the name Beauty 360.

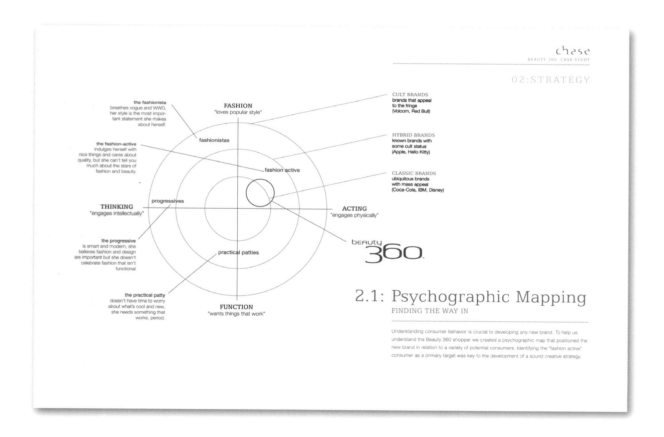

THIS PAGE AND OPPOSITE
Understanding consumer behavior is crucial to
developing any new brand. To help Chase understand
the Beauty 360 shopper, they created a psychographic
map that positioned the new brand in relation to a
variety of potential consumers (opposite). Identifying
the "fashion active"consumer as a primary target was
key to the development of a sound creative strategy.
A "fashion active" consumer persona, or composite
person based on real data, helped the designers clarify
the Beauty 360 brand position (top, right). Mood boards
were created to communicate the fusion of ideas, words,
and images that would resonate best with this consumer
(bottom, right). Together, these materials contained
the guiding principles that informed every design
deliverable for Beauty 360.

Innovation

A new way of doing something is the essence of innovation. Whether
it involves thinking, processes, products, or services, it can involve an
individual or an entire organization. Innovation is an idea, while invention
is about making an idea manifest. Viewed in economic terms, innovation
must increase value to be a success—whether it's incremental or radical.
In artistic terms, often just creating something substantially different
is a successful innovation. In design, it's both.

1.1: The Challenge
IDENTIFY THE BUSINESS PROBLEM

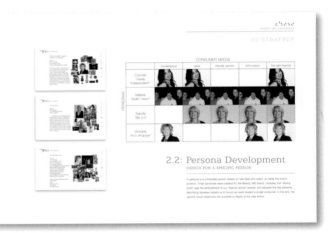

2.2: Persona Development
DESIGN FOR A SPECIFIC PERSON

1.2: Competitive Audit
MARKET RESEARCH

3.1: Visual Brand Stories
SPEAK THE SAME LANGUAGE

The new Beauty 360 logotype evokes a bold, fresh sophistication. A proprietary graphics pattern and clean silver and white palette allowed the retail store to feel like a fresh canvas for a wide variety of beauty brands to stand out. Innovative shopping bags were designed to feature slip-in panels to interchange seasonal graphics and feature special events.

Because beauty retail features small products in a visually busy environment, early development of the store interior and graphic style included large-scale wall coverings and banners to create impact and simplify communication. Large digital prints are mounted to walls around the entryways to grab customers' attention and lead them into the space. A brand guide shows CVS/pharmacy's internal teams how to create support materials with a clear and consistent brand voice.

Full Throttle

When Coca-Cola purchased the Full Throttle brand, they needed a way to expand the line without losing core equities. Chase Design Group was hired to analyze the category and suggest package design options that would allow for expansion and growth. Reviewing the energy drink category revealed it to be an extremely competitive one. It was important to understand exactly what the Full Throttle brand personality was in order to properly position the product.

Mapping the core elements of the Full Throttle visual equity to classic styles and cultural themes helped Chase to recommend design directions consistent with the way consumers felt about the brand. Proposed package designs picked up on familiar elements and iconography to create connections with the original equity. Chase also recommended a system of flavor colors and names that convey an edgy, masculine brand. Strong color and a distinctive pinstripe detailing borrowed from car culture were elements that fit naturally for the classic energy drink.

BELOW
Chase Design Group began work with an audit of the competitive landscape for Full Throttle. The designers created a visual deconstruction of the existing package graphics to identify relevant visual and emotional elements. Identifying how styles and colors contributed to the existing brand allowed the redesign without losing equity.

chase
FULL THROTTLE: CASE STUDY

01:RESEARCH

1.1: The Challenge
IDENTIFY THE BUSINESS PROBLEM

The energy drink category is an extremely competitive one. Coca Cola had recently purchased the Full Throttle brand and needed a way to expand the line without losing core equities. Chase was hired to analyze the category and suggest package design options that would allow for expansion and growth.

Starbucks

Starbucks, the international coffeehouse chain, had been selling coffee-related gift and houseware products for years. Most of these items had a simple logo applied and were not designs created specifically for Starbucks. Chase was hired to create an entirely new program of products that would accurately express the Starbucks brand through shape, materials, color, and pattern. Thorough research allowed the designers to understand core brand equities, an exploration of product trends, and a variety of manufacturing options. Based on these findings, a signature program was developed that included several different design "themes." Each included colors, materials suggestions, product recommendations, and print and icon assets. These themes were designed to be flexible so that assets from different themes could be mixed to create fresh looks. Starbucks signature products include mugs and cups but also extend to include small games, stationery, and home decor, all expressing the core Starbucks brand.

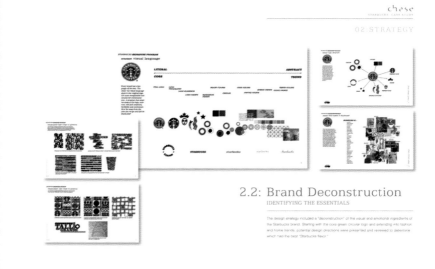

ABOVE
Starting with the client's classic green circular logo and extending into fashion and home trends, potential design directions were presented and reviewed to determine which had the best "Starbucks flavor."

4.1: Assets + Brand Guide
MAPPING THE WAY FORWARD

The design program included several different design "themes." Each included colors, materials suggestions, product recommendations and print and icon assets. The themes were designed to be flexible so that assets from different themes could be mixed to create fresh looks. The final program included a guideline document that would allow Starbucks' in-house team to develop consistently on-brand products using a variety of different vendors and materials.

4.2: Product Collections
CRAFTING THE SOLUTION

Each Signature product line or collection is unique but all reflect the core Starbucks brand character through consistent use of colors, materials and design motifs provided in the guidelines.

Design Supports Internal Communications

Some clients are so busy focusing on their products and services that they neglect their most valuable asset—their employees. If you think of employees, and other stakeholders like investors or the board of directors, as a target audience, it becomes clear that they are also another audience for design. Too often, clients neglect to spend the money to do internal communications well. Graphic design and its enormous ability to communicate well to a variety of people in a range of media is an activity clients should invest in and nurture for their employees as well as their customers. Using design to inform, enlighten, and motivate internal audiences can result in the following:

All the talk and good intentions about creating a culture of innovation will go nowhere without employee buy-in. Design can play a real role in shepherding this critical step. Therefore, design has a significant role with both internal and external audiences.

Also, as CEOs of companies and organizations find themselves in the public eye—either in person or online—they need the power of design to assist them, making their presentations into compelling audiovisual shows. The thinking, skills, and methodologies used to develop a package design should be used for PowerPoint presentation support slides as well. All of these things should be consistent. Once again, it is about controlling all design touchpoints.

Design

- Clarity of goal definition
- Alignment of goals to actions
- Connection of staff to CEO vision and charisma
- Increase participation and empowerment
- Aid in recruitment and retention
- Boost communication and advocacy
- Elevate leadership and organizational management
- Monitor results in these areas

Project Profile in Big Goals: Employee Communications
Sun Microsystems, Inc. designed by The Fibonacci Design Group, LLC. / Los Angeles, California USA

The Fibonacci Design Group specializes in marketing and creative strategy for print and web design. Partners and cocreative directors, Gregory and Sloane Mann have a breadth of experience in employee communication design. Their work on internal communications for multinational technology and computer network giant, Sun Microsystems, quantifies the intangibles of Sun's culture through the development of a proprietary visual language. The grammar of this language is built on the employee value proposition and positive team member experiences. "The campaign engaged and motivated the team to 'live the brand,'" says Sloane Mann. "Our work on this campaign focused on the strengths and beliefs already developed for Sun's brand expression and couple that with a healthy dose of irreverence and fun." For this campaign, a brochure, video, and CEO presentation were designed. The results were impressive: out of the 400 companies that applied for the award, Sun Microsystems was ranked as the fifth best place to work in California by the Great Place to Work Institute.

TOP
Internal employee branding, such as the brochure shown below, increased Sun's perceived value by engendering pride in the employees.

BOTTOM
The campaign was used extensively for presentation purposes by top Sun Microsystems executives at both internal and external meetings.

Case Study in Big Goals: Globalization
Weiden+Kennedy / Tokyo, Japan

Weiden+Kennedy (W+K) is one of the largest independently owned advertising agencies in the world. It came to prominence in the 1980s with its iconic work for Nike, including the "Just Do It" tagline. Founded in Portland, Oregon, the agency now has offices In New York City, London, Amsterdam, Delhi, Shanghai, Beijing, and Tokyo. With a mission to that create strong and provocative relationships between good companies and their consumers, they are one of the most award-winning agencies in the world. They also understand how to serve global brands, maintaining the core of the brand while evolving it to meet the needs of the various cultures around the world. The Tokyo office says of itself: "We are not a Japanese agency. Nor are we a branch of a Western agency doing adaptation work. W+K is a hybrid—mixing different cultures, interests, backgrounds, and skills to bring a new perspective, expertise, and level of creativity to brand building for companies in Japan."

Google

"The OOH [Out Of Home or outdoor advertising], online ads, YouTube videos and mobile ads take users to the *dekirukoto* website where people can learn more about Google through tutorials that illustrate their products in a 'Googly' way," explains W+K Tokyo creative director, Eric Cruz.

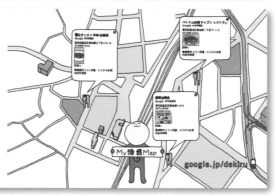

LEFT
Google is known for search, but what many people don't know is that there are literally hundreds of ways you can search with Google to find exactly what you're looking for. To showcase the many ways Google can be a useful tool in people's everyday lives, W+K developed a campaign using a friendly and colorful illustration style to communicate *Google de dekirukoto* (or "Things you can do with Google"). The Japan campaign features useful search tips, ranging from using Google's mobile movie search to finding movie times and locations, to using Google Earth to travel to the Eiffel Tower, to finding your way to a local ramen shop using Google Street View, strategically placed in high-traffic train and metro stations throughout Japan. The campaign also included live events.

Globalization

Globalization is the process of uniting all the people of the world into a single society. It is a term that has been used since the 1960s and often refers to economic globalization in which nations contribute to an increasingly international economy through trade, investment, migration, and the spread of technology. More than economics, globalization is also driven by a combination of political, technological, cultural and biological factors. In design, globalization means the transnational dissemination of ideas, language, and pop culture. It's about breaking down barriers between people and sharing through a common, often visual, language.

DJ Uppercut

Based out of the Tokyo office, W+K Tokyo Lab is a record label and creative workshop. It has released CD/DVD titles that combine music, graphics, and films featuring local hip-hop and electronic artists that have become a sensation around the world, uniting people. The W+K Tokyo Lab artist roster includes Hifana, Takagi Masakatsu, Afra and DJ Uppercut, whose music video stills are seen here.

Nike

W+K has a long and successful relationship with athletic shoe and equipment manufacturer, Nike. "This is Love" is the first "Just Do It" women's campaign for Asia Pacific. Targeted to Asian women aged 19 to 21, the goal was to convey the exhilaration of sport and the role it plays in their everyday lives. Through the lens of dance, kickboxing, basketball, and volleyball, the ads celebrate the drive, passion, and commitment of young women across the region and the feeling sport creates, much like falling in love.

BOTTOM

Football in Asia is in dire need of players like Cristiano Ronaldo and Fernando Torres, who believe they can change the game with every touch of the ball. "Ignite" is a call to action for all Asian footballers to make an impact each and every time they step on the pitch—to inspire them to not only take risks but also take responsibility to influence the game. The broadcast features Nike athletes in a Manchester United vs. Arsenal game and a viral film of Ronaldo's amazing plays as told through three diehard fans. Print/OOH highlights how Nike's innovative products help the athletes' performance.

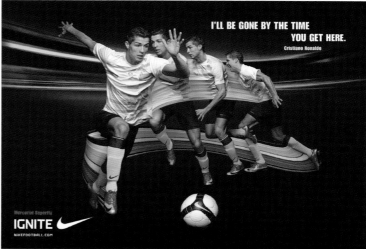

Jemapur

"Maledict Car" is the first single from new artist, Jemapur. This music video, directed by Kosai Sekine, is the tenth release of W+K Tokyo Lab. In kanji, the idea of "ten" [十] means point or dot, and this video captures a very unique viewpoint of Tokyo through an intricate visual montage of points and patterns of geometric cityscapes. It also features some of the surreal characters that dwell within those spaces. Through its disorientation and choice of imagery, this video also conveys what Jemapur refers to as "moving forward through a door, only to find oneself back in the same place again."

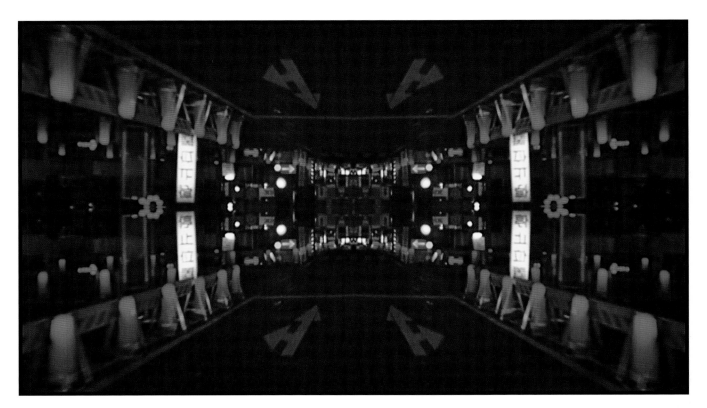

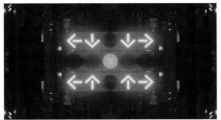

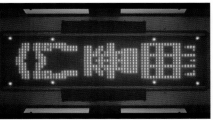

Socially Responsible Design

Whether the goal is crossing cultures and uniting people through globalization or motivating and supporting environmental consciousness and sustainability, an understanding of various changing contexts is important for successful design. Designers need to be socially responsible in the broadest sense of the term, essentially, using their powers for good. Some things to consider:

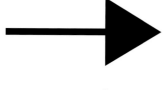

Awareness:
Observe the current situation and emerging trends through the filter of cultural differences.

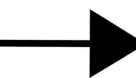

Sensitivity:
Adapt and evolve to meet the preferences and behaviors of different audiences.

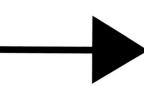

Integration:
New expressions that work to create desired perceptions may not look the same for different audiences.

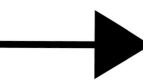

Assessment:
Create advocacy teams and communication groups that provide feedback that expresses the values and needs of the audience.

Verification:
Look at consumption patterns and relate user experiences to goals. Determine if the audience is served and if there is a tangible benefit to all.

Project Profile in Big Goals: Sustainability

Nickelodeon Magazine **Illustrations designed by Jessica Hische / Brooklyn, New York USA**

***Nickelodeon Magazine* Illustrations**

Jessica Hische, a designer/illustrator in Brooklyn, draws type, editorial illustrations, and designs pretty things. For the April issue of *Nickelodeon Magazine*, a companion to the children's television network, Hische created Pro-Environment Seed Packets for plants that don't currently exist, but would help make the world a greener place. The creative brief from magazine senior designer, Caitlin Keegans, reads: *Venus Can Trap*

(*Aluminus Devouris*): The only flower that eats metal. Never needs watering. Keep cell phones, iPods, loose change, helicopters, and aluminum siding away from plant.
The Power Plant (*Voltagius Florus*): This gorgeous perennial will brighten up your home … literally. It's easy, just plant your Power Plant, water it, and in a month all your electrical needs will be taken care of. The long graceful petals accept AC/DC plugs. Keep away from bathtubs, pools, and peeing

dogs. *Rainshower Flower* (*Delugius Irrigatius Maximus*): This glorious, powerful hybrid of the sunflower is perfect for the desert or any dry clime. Plant grows to 100 feet tall and then continually erupts in refreshing, fragrant rainfall. Great for watering farmland and for refilling empty bottles of expensive water. Guaranteed to keep fields moist, rivers flowing, and shoes soaked. Plant in area with proper drainage.

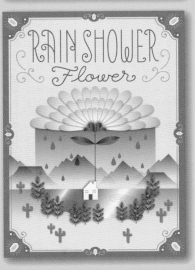

Case Study in Big Goals: Sustainability

smashLAB / Vancouver, BC, Canada

Vancouver-based smashLAB is an interaction design studio directed by partners Eric Shelkie, who plans and codes, and Eric Karjaluoto, who does strategy and design. The firm builds websites both for themselves and clients. "People tell us that we've really helped them focus and spread the word," says Karjaluoto. "We think this is in part because we're small; as such, there's no bureaucracy here. Our clients get direct access to the people who actually do the work, and they seem to find that refreshing." SmashLAB helps clients leverage technology, but also works with them on the positioning of their organizations, developing marketing strategies, many of which revolve in some way around sustainability and social responsibility.

Design Can Change

Design Can Change is a self-directed project undertaken and financed completely by smashLAB. It was born from a frustration with the lack of information available related to sustainability and graphic design. The paper and pulp industry is the world's third largest polluter. According to the AIGA, their members alone specify or purchase $9.1 billion in printing and paper annually. In seeking ways to help mitigate their impact,

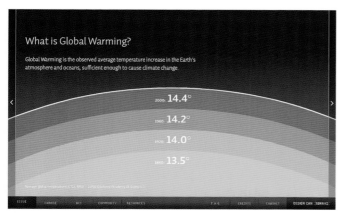

smashLAB found few resources directly related to graphic design. "We sought to create a resource that would serve as a comprehensible first-step for designers wishing to embrace more sustainable practices. Additionally, Design Can Change aimed to unite the world's graphic designers to use their influence and purchasing power to combat climate change," explains smashLAB creative director, Karjaluoto.

BELOW
SmashLAB worked to simplify complex data into dynamic and digestible pieces. As a result, the site is Flash-based and linear, allowing visitors to move through it like a slide show The volume of text was edited heavily in order to maintain user interest; similarly, animated information graphics added visual representations of the data provided. Site color was mostly neutral grays and creams, with a hot red that is used to activate certain areas and harkens to the alert-like nature of the subject matter. Navigation elements are largely tucked away, maximizing usable space for content. Thousands of designers have taken the Design Can Change pledge, committing to more sustainable practices. In addition, Design Can Change was recognized in *Time* magazine's Design 100.

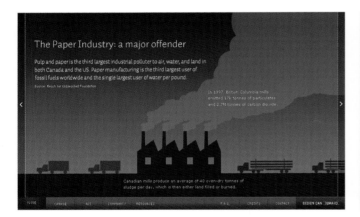

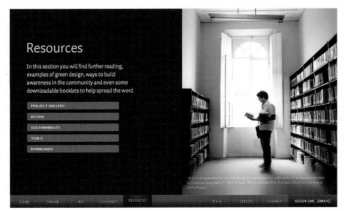

Ascent

Ascent is a company with two divisions: a charter helicopter service that provides specialized flight services for mining exploration, aerial construction, fire fighting and heli-skiing. Additionally, they run a startup aerospace company that designs and manufactures specialized aeronautic equipment for both government and industry. SmashLAB was tasked with crafting an identity and website that worked for both divisions. The resulting design conveys the notion of "exclusivity" and infused an elegant and refined aesthetic. Bold statements and clear messaging exude the confidence that comes from experience and success, while aspirational imagery illustrates the mythic and majestic nature of flying.

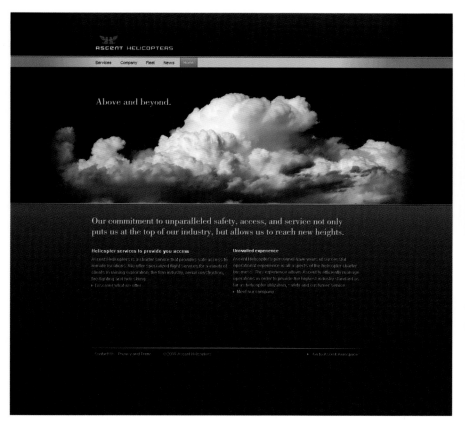

Borealis

Borealis is a voluntary carbon-offset provider that creates and manages forests to store CO_2. Realizing the destructive magnitude of a mountain pine beetle infestation, the Borealis consortium of eleven forest-management consultancies and businesses was formed to create mitigation and response strategies for sustaining the forest products industry and local communities through the crisis. SmashLAB designed an unexpected brand identity and an information-focused website for the consortium. The visual treatments are informed by the Aurora Borealis, a naturally occurring light phenomenon in the sky at the Earth's poles. They are conveyed through a series of concentric circles that almost come to life by way of an optical illusion, and augmented by the deep, rich colors found in the Aurora Borealis.

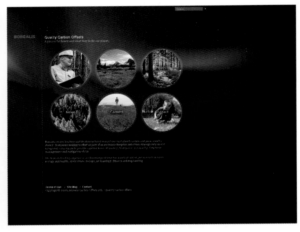

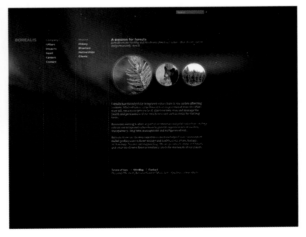

Northern British Columbia Tourism

Northern BC's vast wilderness comprises more than half the province—approximately 193,051 square miles (500,000 sq km)—twice the size of the U.K. Northern BC Tourism markets this vast region to visitors. SmashLAB completely rebranded the organization with a new identity, printed collateral, presentation materials, website, and ad campaign. The ads feature a somewhat irreverent take on bear-safety notifications while showcasing the area's stunning backdrops. "We intended to break away from some of the more tired tourism imagery, and the man in the bear suit helps accomplish this," says smashLAB creative director, Karjaluoto.

SEI: The Green Report Card

The SEI (The Sustainable Endowments Institute) College Sustainability Report Card is the only independent evaluation of colleges and universities that are leading by example in their commitment to sustainability. To extend its usefulness and reach, the client needed to offer a clear and concise online tool that would welcome users with readily accessible information. "They felt that they had to be increasingly transparent with

Bear Safety Tip 31: While in Northern BC, keep an eye on your pets. Bears and pets usually don't get along very well.

Plan a real (and safe) northern adventure today: 1.800.663.8843
Background: Monkman Falls (courtesy of Tourism BC/Albert Normandin)
See what else is waiting for you: www.northernbctourism.com

Bear Safety Tip 28: In the event of a black bear attack, fight back using sticks, rocks, or whatever else is available.

Plan a real (and safe) northern adventure today: 1.800.663.8843
Background: Red Fern Lake (courtesy of Tourism BC/Albert Normandin)
See what else is waiting for you: www.northernbctourism.com

regards to how their grading system works in order to cement the credibility of their data," explains Karjaluoto. "They also wanted to streamline the cumbersome method in which they compiled data in the field." The new site facilitates data collection, while allowing users to easily browse and compare massive amounts of data.

BELOW
The site positions SEI as "the definitive voice on college sustainability." The design leverages the authority and trust established by the report card with academic motifs, resulting in a credible, yet accessible, tone. The implication is that the organization takes a methodical approach to gathering data and assessments, pays attention to detail, and possesses the skills required to produce such a report. Elegantly crafted botanical illustrations are used on key pages, and colors are muted, allowing images and interface elements to take precedence. Typography is treated simply with headings in a serif face and body copy in a sans serif, striking a balance between classic and contemporary sensibilities. Most of the type is HTML-based to keep load times to a minimum.

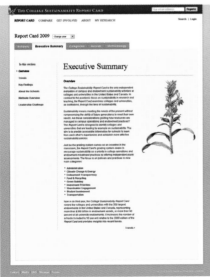

Sustainability

Sustainability, at least as it is commonly referred to in design, means responsible use of natural resources. When managed properly, it allows social, business, and ecological concerns to work in productive relationship to each other. All of it in order to support the long-term well being of humans, animals, and nature. Sustainability is a goal that impacts all life on the planet and is, therefore, a global initiative.

Measuring Design

Designers are always working on building trust with their clients. In order to work toward meeting the many challenges our planet faces, or simply helping businesses create better relationships with their customers, designers need to be valued and respected. It would be great if designers could use traditional business management metrics to measure design's contribution to a client's bottom line. This becomes even more difficult to assess with graphic design in particular. Some design is more measurable than others; obviously websites are a great example. The "soft measure" design disciplines like corporate identity are far harder to measure.

Many international design organizations such as the nationally funded U.K. Design Council and Danish Design Center, as well as the privately held American-based Design Management Institute, work constantly to research and report on the value of design. The data and case studies they collect are not always black and white evidence of design's financial impact.

Factors to Assess

There are a number of ways to look at design's value. There are quantitative (having a measurable property) and qualitative (possessing a high degree of subjectivity) factors to examine and analyze.

Some things to look at when measuring design's quantitative contribution:
• Process improvement
• Overall cost savings
• Reduction in materials and waste
• User/community interaction
• New market adoption

Some qualitative things to look at:
• Customer satisfaction
• Brand reputation
• Increased aesthetic appeal
• Improved functionality

The Triple Bottom Line

The most accurate, effective, and relevant measurements for design tend to be an evaluation of both the tangible and intangible benefits to a business or organization. Trying to discern design's direct impact on sales is often very difficult to quantify. These days, most companies tend to look at what is coming to be known as "the triple bottom line." That is, accounting for the social, environmental, and business impact of their products and services. Therefore, clients tend to measure design's interaction with these factors and balance to evaluate results holistically.

Design's lasting value comes in encouraging behavior that our client seeks to affect. By helping inform, persuade, and motivate, design works to get audiences to think and do what the client wants. If this objective is geared toward the social responsibility of the triple bottom line, or an increase in revenue, design plays a valuable role.

The Triple Bottom Line

Design can play a critical role in supporting sustainability efforts. All three important factors involved in sustainability problem solving and decision making: social, economic, and environment. Design solutions must balance this triple bottom line to truly achieve sustainability.

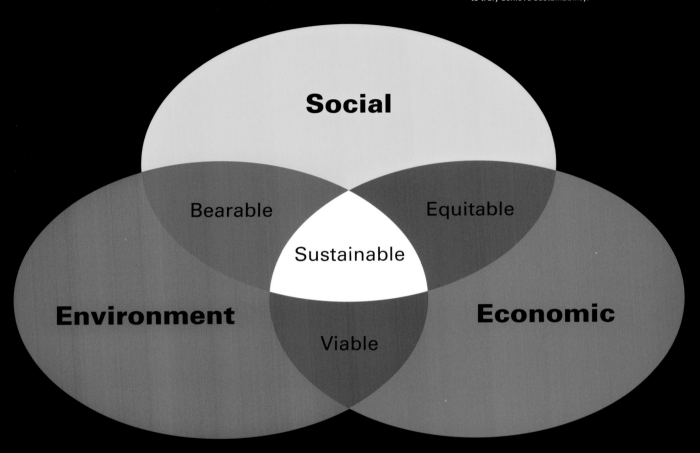

Making the Most of Design Investment

Do the right job
Don't think a new logo can solve a customer service problem. Investigate the real problems and respond accordingly. Take time framing or focusing the issue and developing the assignment.

Understand the audience
Design for the right people using the right approach. Don't waste time and money trying to force a bad idea on the audience.

Focus
Make less stuff, do fewer design projects, but do them better. Limit efforts.

Organize revisions
So much waste occurs by not gathering all responses at critical decision points in the design process. It's better to have fewer batches of revisions that include everyone's input.

Hire the right designer
Make sure the team is composed of people with the skills and talent required for the project.

Case Study in Experiential Branding

Imaginary Forces / Los Angeles, California • New York, New York USA

Design leadership is essential to any and all branding activities. Developing and maintaining a successful brand takes persistent vision. Branding is often confused with identity design (i.e., logo, trade dress, etc), when it is really about storytelling. More accurately, branding is creating a story about a product or service that will form in the minds of an audience. To accomplish that, designers employ everything from appropriate typographic choices to selecting the best delivery media to suggesting the right celebrity spokesperson for their clients. It's all about creating impressions and connections with an audience. In that sense, all brand design is experienced. As people become savvier about how they are marketed to, and marketplace competition increases, the need for true differentiation and authentic experience as a branding tool becomes very significant. Effective design management in branding means utilizing all available delivery media—increasingly, that means experience design.

MoMA Digital Display

The Museum of Modern Art (MoMA) in New York City is a place that fuels creativity, ignites minds, and provides inspiration. With extraordinary exhibitions and one of the world's finest collections of modern and contemporary art, MoMA is dedicated to the conversation between the past and the present, the established and the experimental. Their mission is helping us to understand and enjoy the art of our time.

Imaginary Forces worked with MoMA to create a digital fingerprint of the new MoMA in Manhattan. Nine separate screens provide content on events, exhibitions, art, and commerce; while a theatrical transitional curtain works to reveal the museum's digital collection, providing both intriguing information and adding to the ambience. IF's work adds to the museum guests' experience by helping them navigate the many enjoyable aspects of their visit to MoMA.

OPPOSITE AND BELOW
The Museum of Modern Art in midtown Manhattan is one of the most influential and important museums of contemporary art in the world. IF created a visitor experience that orientates, informs, and entertains via nine digital screens.

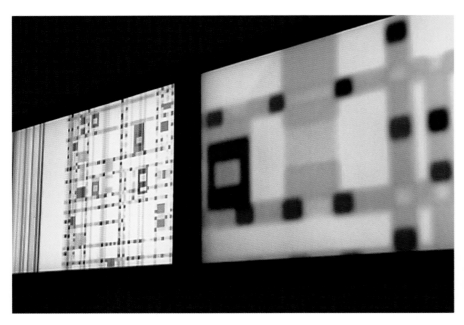

Experience Design

As experience design becomes more prevalent in society, it begs the question, what exactly *is* experience design? There isn't a simple definition. The evolution of technology has changed the way we interact with the world. This evolution has led to the orchestration of media and architecture to create spaces that inform and inspire. The creators of experience design projects seamlessly integrate cinematic storytelling, interactive content, emerging technologies, and innovative architecture. These disciplines converge to meet a basic human need: connection.

Victoria's Secret Fashion Show

Drawing celebrities and millions of viewers each year, the annual Victoria's Secret Fashion Show features some of the world's most beautiful and best-paid models in elaborately costumed lingerie—the showstopper being a multimillion dollar "Fantasy Bra." This event boasts music, special performances, and extravagant set designs that complement multiple themes running within the show. Imaginary Forces (IF) directed and designed the projected imagery and broadcast graphics for the 2008 Victoria's Secret Fashion Show. The entire show was staged in a temporary structure that was constructed in front of the legendary Fontainbleau Hotel. Seamlessly integrated into this architecture were fifteen giant kinetic projection screens that served as a dynamic backdrop. Choreographed to the show, the content projected on these screens was a mix of motion graphics, photo-real animation, live action and visual effects all created by IF under the creative direction of Grant Lau.

BELOW
In collaboration with production company Done and Dusted and fashion staging company OBO, IF transformed the architectural environment into a living theatrical backdrop, painted with animated colors and shapes and packaged with integrated broadcast graphics for CBS television network's airing of the fashion show.

Wynn Las Vegas Aquatic Extravaganza

Imaginary Forces (IF) contributed its expertise to Wynn Las Vegas, the $2.7 billion resort and casino from impresario Stephen A. Wynn. The visual centerpiece of the resort is the 1-acre, man-made lake called the Lake of Dreams, an essential part of a colorful outdoor multimedia theatrical show. This production is complete with animatronic creatures, choreographed dance performances, and vibrant graphics. Under project direction by Todd Nisbet and creative direction by Kenny Ortega, IF created content and visuals for the show, which are projected onto an enormous 40-foot waterfall screen, as well as on a circular display that rises above the larger screen. The whole setting changes from fire to ice with a groundbreaking technology that is a closely guarded secret. Lighting design by Patrick Woodruff and set/prop design by Michael Curry completed the project.

BELOW
"Our goal was to conceptualize and pull visual references to make the worlds more fantastical and impressive," explains Imaginary Forces creative director Karin Fong. "We maintained some tension between the elements—essentially creating an environment that comes alive via the animatronic props, screens and blowing silks." The animations used in the show were done with cell, handmade techniques, and CG. Compositing was achieved in Flame and Inferno, with editing done using Final Cut Pro.

Imaginary Forces (IF), highly regarded for their continued work on Hollywood feature films, commercial branding, and television content, is at the forefront of the experience design movement. The design agency, based in New York and Los Angeles, is also constructing a growing following among world-renowned architectural firms including: Frank Gehry, Foreign Office Architects, UN Studio, Diller + Scofidio, Greg Lynn/FORM, Gensler, George Yu Architects, Reiser + Umemoto, and KPF, among others.

Ground Zero Redesign

Imaginary Forces (IF) joined United Architects—a multidisciplinary, multinational consortium of architects, planners, and designers—to become one of the six finalists selected to present a design for the redevelopment of ground zero, the former World Trade Center site in New York City.

The group represented an alternative voice of a younger generation that grasps modernism in the fullest sense of the term. IF's collaboration was under the creative direction of New York–based former IF partner, Mikon van Gastel. The Dutch-born van Gastel's recent projects include environmental designs for IBM's Center for e-business Innovation in Chicago and a massive video display with 24-hour content for a skyscraper in New York's Times Square. The IF team all agreed the only way to approach a project of this significance architecturally and emotionally is to be unconventional. Traditional development to hallowed ground did not seem appropriate or possible. We explored the idea of utopia—of a space that embraces progress in all areas of life, work, play, and remembrance.

A Special Memorial

The United Architects team created a plan for the entire site as a monument to the American tragedy of September 11, as well as a new vision for a thriving public and commercial space, as it once had been. A series of five interconnected buildings that enclose a cathedral-like space dominate the 16-acre

site. A vast public plaza and park is formed around the connected tower buildings. The plan calls for preserving the original World Trade Center footprint with a memorial placed below ground level in the footprint designed to direct visitors' gazes upwards in remembrance. In addition, a Sky Memorial atop the first tower allows visitors to look down over the ground where so many lost their lives. Beyond the memorial, the plan includes shops, offices, conference centers, restaurants, spas, sports and entertainment centers, and numerous gardens in over 10.5 million square feet (975,482 m²), and over 1,620 feet (494 m) tall (approximately 112 floors) in the highest tower.

Guiding and Visualizing

Illuminating this "City in the Sky" concept, capturing the essence of the plan while conveying both the memorial and lively aspects of the design was a challenge. It is a bold and unusual schematic, also designed with safety in mind given the site's history. All of these things needed to be successfully expressed and then grasped by a judging committee for the Lower Manhattan Development Corporation and the Port Authority of New York, who acted as clients in this project.

Creating Moments

The Design Council, the UK's national strategic organization for design, says that initial considerations for experiential engagement are not based on what messages to communicate and what media should be used to carry them. Rather, they advise us to think about what could make a great brand/consumer "moment." The questions to ask are

- Where would it be?
- What would it involve?
- How would it be staged?
- How would it be remembered?
- How would it be retold?

OPPOSITE
Conveying the experience of a redevelopment plan for the Lower Manhattan site of the September 11th tragedy challenged Imaginary Forces (IF) to help the client understand what it would be like to be in the new spaces. IF worked as a core member of the United Architects team to conceptualize and communicate the design's goals and the plan's specifics. As part of the team's presentation, IF also designed a short film to show the full integration of the experience within lower Manhattan. They also helped build an exhibit to showcase the design at the Winter Garden in New York City.

LEFT
Imaginary Forces (IF) cofounder Peter Frankfurt notes, "If you look at IF's background in designing opening title sequences for feature films, it is essentially a history of storytelling—setting a mood for what people are about to experience visually, intellectually, and emotionally. For us to be involved in the storytelling of the rebuilding effort in downtown Manhattan is both thrilling and humbling."

IF collaborated with United Architects, a creative consortium that included five cutting edge architectural firms: Reiser + Umemoto, RUR Architecture (New York), Foreign Office Architects (London), Greg Lynn FORM (Los Angeles), Kevin Kennon Architect (New York) and UN Studio (Amsterdam).

Chapter 3
Design-Centric Research

The Importance of Research for Design

The best design is nearly always informed by some kind of research. At its best, research gives designers insights into the human, cultural, technical, emotional, and cognitive factors in a domain or context that they are designing for. However, some research studies can lead to erroneous conclusions and mistaken concepts.

Most designers at some point in their careers, have been handed a research report or "deck" from the client—usually from the marketing department. Valuable time and money has been spent acquiring this information, and the designer is expected to make use of it. Some of these decks are amazing, while others seem to be silly, almost futile, exercises. A designer can look at one of these reports and reach conclusions completely different from the researchers. It comes down to how you look at it. You'll find that designers who place strong value on using research to inform their thinking, typically do their own studies. Sometimes, even duplicating the client's efforts.

Research Methods

Context is critical to design, and it is critical to the research that aids design. However, exactly which type of research to employ is often debated by clients and designers. Over the years, different research methods have been in favor, including the following.

Traditional Market Research

Broadly speaking, market research is any organized effort to gather information about customers. Some methods traditionally used include

- **Demographics: looking at quantifiable statistical data that describes a group of people or target market segment.**
- **Focus groups: where a group of people from the target market are led in a discussion to solicit opinions and reactions.**
- **Psychographics: a means of evaluating subjective beliefs, preferences, and opinions. It seeks to determine why people do what they do.**

Ethnographic Research

Ethnography is a type of research rooted in anthropology that looks at the links between culture and human behavior. Viewed both from a group's or individual's perspective, these research observations describe people based on thought, behavior, and actions. Some methods include

- **Observational research views and records behavior without interacting with or questioning people.**
- **Visual anthropology allows a trained researcher to photograph or review photos and visual reference materials in order to draw conclusions about people.**
- **Photo ethnology requires that the people being studied photograph or record themselves, revealing their preferences and behaviors.**

User Experience Research

This type of research measures the ability of a product or service to meet the needs of the end-user. Sometimes called "testing" or "usability testing," it lets researchers view behavior directly. Some methods include

- **Observational research views and records people as they interact with a product or service. Often used as validation for design concepts.**
- **Web analytics track users behavior on a website using quantitative metrics built into the site. These statistics measure a set of variables and illustrate the user interaction with website content.**
- **Personas are a theoretical method of developing hypothetical users for a product or service that springs from the discipline of interactive design. An archetype or hypothetical perfect user is created, then their motivations, lifestyles, and expectations are examined.**

Classic Design Research

Mostly, information gathered first-hand by the designer through visual review and subjective analysis. Methods include

- Visual audits: review of client and/or competitor products and services plus their related designed materials, in situ. Observations are typically photographed.
- **Prototype testing: creating iterations of a design, making a mock-up or prototype, using it, and making refinements as necessary.**
- **Participation: the designer personally experiences the product or service for themselves and records impressions and insights.**

Blended Research

Some form of subjective and objective, qualitative and quantitative, field and lab methods are used. Typically, a little bit of each of the research methodologies listed above is completed and analyzed.

Case Study in Design-Centric Research
Culture Advertising Design / Atlanta, Georgia USA

Culture AD has been providing services in the field of advertising and design since 2001. The agency parses the aesthetic and strategic aspects of graphic design and combines them with the experience and insights of advertising to create relevant visual, tactical, and vital marketing tools. Headed by creative director Craig Brimm, their work targets African Americans as well as general-market consumers. Culture AD's approach to design is about moving brands ahead through relevant concepts and visuals. Brimm says, "Today's society is moving so fast, and we receive messages so quickly and frequently, that it is essential for brands to evolve so they do not fall victim to circumstance." To inform their work, the agency brings creativity, market insights, and human behavior expertise.

African Pride

African Pride is a beauty brand within Colomer USA. Formerly Revlon Professional Products, Colomer USA makes and markets a variety of heath and beauty products, specializing in ethnic hair care primarily marketed to African American and Hispanic consumers. Over the years, African Pride had many improvements to its relaxer formula, as well as expanded its hair-care maintenance offerings. Culture AD was tasked with creating a package design, which

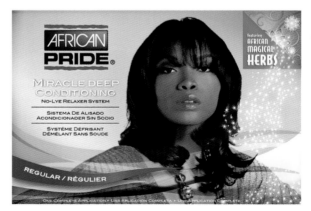

was a portion of a brand restaging that also included print advertising, a thirty-second theater commercial, and a seven-minute in-store promotional video. The target audience is African American women ages eighteen to twenty-five years old. "Our approach was to add a little sophistication to a market that is often under valued for it's savvy and knowledgeable pursuit of hair-care products," explains Brimm. "This distinct market is avid in their research and conversations about hair, hair health, hair care and product selection. All of this led to creating packaging and advertising that didn't pander to the lowest common themes. Instead, we took the path that met them where their psychographic profile said their understanding was best acclimated. That was to offer full disclosure of natural ingredients, inherent properties of said ingredients, and ultimate hair health and styling benefits." The resulting design has a youthful, vibrant look.

Urban Intelligence: itsTMI.com

Urban Intelligence is a video production and digital music distribution company that also owns and runs www.itsTMI.com, the urban youth news/gossip website. The owner, Terrance Moore III, is a college-aged entrepreneur, who gathers, records, presents, narrates, and discusses the site's content. Culture AD's challenge was to create an identity and website that melds two separate businesses into one cohesively branded entity. "To do this," Brimm says, "allow for experimentation of visual elements and the natural evolution of the brand's iterations."

Readers Make Leaders

Trying to reach urban teenagers and convince them of the value of reading is the mission of the nonprofit literacy group, Readers Make Leaders. The organization needed a brand identity that would present a more professional image to donors, as well as catch the eye of the children it served. "The target market was urban high school students ages fourteen to nineteen years old," notes Culture AD agency manager, Brooke Brimm. "We know this demographic to be vastly underestimated as far as the intellect, habits, and collective consciousness. They are intimately aware of their surroundings, the way they are perceived, as well as their enormous power and influence on world culture." Culture AD's design co-opts fashion trends, imbuing relevant iconography with a relaxed sense of excellence.

Creme of Nature

Creme of Nature Professional is another brand of the Colomer Group, the international health and beauty product company. Well-established in the ethnic hair care industry, Creme of Nature Professional products have been sold for over thirty years to hair care professionals, as well as home-application consumers. Culture AD created point of purchase, public relations materials, and a poster, which was also adapted as a print advertising campaign, targeted to African American women ages twenty-five to fifty-five years old. "Ethnic hair care is one of the most dense, complicated, and misunderstood marketing category in existence today," says Brimm. "The marketplace is fraught with issues as complex as battling urban myths and incorrect assumptions to multiple brands with questionable efficacies and crowded shelves with inconsistent product placement.

The messaging in ethnic hair care has to be more than direct. It must be laser focused while being markedly honest. We had to do more than allude to natural ingredients. We had to verify the quality of those ingredients and underscore their level of purity." As a result, the design expresses reliability and commitment to healthy hair.

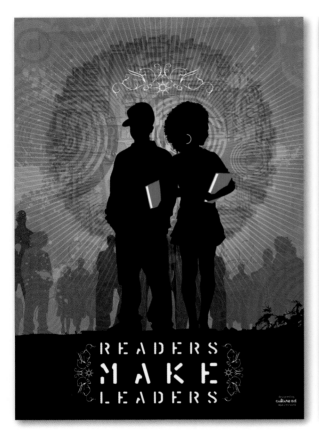

Research Aligns and Focuses Design

The scale and complexity of the design research typically depends on several factors. The more research available to a designer, the better their decision making can be.

Key Factors for Deciding Research Method

The research method, as well as the scope of this research, typically depends on several things:

- Client's category of product or service
- Budget
- What is being researched
- Number of people being studied
- Time frame

Typically, it is the large consumer product categories that invest the most resources into research, because of the vast amounts of money invested overall. While boutique service companies spend the least, perhaps because they are often more personally involved with their customers and feel they already understand them.

Ways to Look at Research

Research is considered to be either

- Quantitative, which measures objective numerical, or fact-based, data; or
- Qualitative, which focuses on subjective data, like thoughts, feelings, motivation, and other qualities that describe people.

In addition, research can be

- Primary, which is information that is gained directly and is commissioned by the client for this purpose; or
- Secondary, which is information obtained indirectly by studying existing data from a variety of sources.

Designers use both or either. It depends on their individual practices whether or not they are involved in commissioning research studies. At the very least, they all do their own observational research of a cursory nature when they study the existing client branding and literature, try to buy or use the product/service, and check out what the competition is doing.

Visualizing Research

Creating pie charts, diagrams, and comparison tables allows both designer and client to make sense of the information. What do they find useful? What is not? These things become more apparent when diagrammed.

Why Research Matters

Research facilitates and focuses design. This is important because through organized investigation, clients and designers can define and understand the following:

- The actual problem
- Realistic objectives
- The context
- The consumer/audience
- Purchasing decisions
- Behavior/use
- The competition
- Verbal/visual language

All of this helps designers make better concepts and improve on the design process by streamlining their explorations. The many design possibilities can effectively be narrowed down, allowing better-informed design direction that ultimately speed workflow. Good research helps eliminate bad, or simply wrong, design concepts.

Project Profile in Design-Centric Research
Supermarket designed by Citizen Scholar, Inc. / Brooklyn, New York USA

Supermarket is a curated online marketplace where shoppers can find high-quality design products and buy them directly from the designers. It is founded, designed, and run by Ryan Duessing and Randy J. Hunt of Supercorp. In addition to Supercorp, Hunt is also creative director of Citizen Scholar, Inc., a Brooklyn-based design consultancy that designs for people who shape society in positive ways.

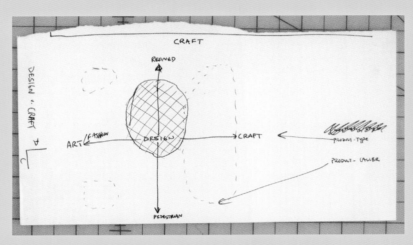

"Our goal, from the beginning, was to make it easy and fun to find and buy great design. Supermarket was a new business, a new website, and a new product idea. As a business, it is an evolution of ideas that started with Ryan Deussing's prior venture as a successful design and gift e-commerce retailer.

"For shoppers, we aimed to create a friendly, authentic experience, free of artifice, where they felt like part of a community without being filled with web gimmicks of the moment. We wanted a marketplace where you'd stick around and come back because of great products and a curator-like point of view. Browsing design products should feel like a creative act, one of discovery.

"For designers, we wanted to create an environment they would be proud to be a part of. Like a good boutique, carefully selected products raise the quality of the experience, and designers want their products to be a part of something like that. By virtue of aggregating individual designer's traffic and visibility, we aimed to craft a rising tide scenario, where each person's success and visibility helps the marketplace as a whole.

"For ourselves, we were pursuing a new business model, that built on the strengths and weaknesses learned from past experience, and allowed us to take advantage of both technological and personal networks to connect more people with high-quality designer's products."

— Supermarket cofounder Randy J. Hunt

BELOW AND RIGHT
Screen captures of www.supermarkethq.com, along with an initial brand positioning concept sketch.

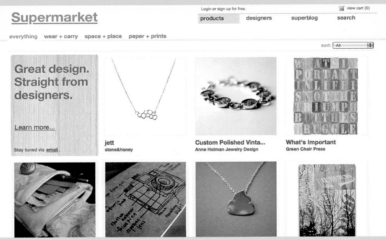

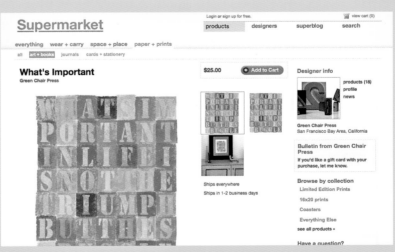

"Beyond our unique curatorial voice, Supermarket also places a very high emphasis on drop-dead ease of use for both shoppers and sellers. That permeates every form, every link, every help page throughout our marketplace. The design of Supermarket is built to serve shoppers' interests and designers' needs. The intersection of those two groups of people is at the heart of the products themselves.

"Product photography is an extremely important part of any online shopping experience, and that's even more true in a highly aesthetic space like design products. We created a design that lets the products take the lead.

"We don't need to pound people over the head with our logo—they'll remember Supermarket because it's the first place to go to find great design products. The logo itself is Helvetica Neue, carefully kerned with a 'designerly' attention to detail. It's underlined as if to say, this is really super. The type choice is based on three major qualities of Helvetica:

• Familiarity (we're not trying to steal the thunder from the products or the designers)
• Its natural comfort with Arial, which is our web-friendly font of choice
• Its associations with 'design-y' things

"Our typography and composition is quite restrained, so it becomes important that the soft, earthy tan acts as a neutral backdrop for the design imagery without feeling cold and impersonal like gray would, but every once in a while there are subtle woodgrain details. These are a nod to warm, solid, authentic materials, like a wood frame on a nice art print or a solid dining table. Beyond the core color palette, use of color is very restrained, and is employed almost exclusively for communicating specific domains of information or points of interaction. For example, all of the shopper FAQs are blue, while the seller FAQs are green.

"Animation and transition effects are employed only at key interaction points that require extra communication or attention, for example, a designer uploading files or saving billing information."
— Supermarket cofounder Randy J. Hunt

"We're entering year number three and our goals are maturing. We're seeing new opportunities and we'll be designing the experience accordingly, " says Hunt. "Ignoring the hyperactivity of the holiday seasons, traffic and sales grow by five to ten percent each month. We consistently hear from both shoppers and sellers how easy it is to use Supermarket and how much they enjoy it. The most satisfying feedback is when we receive emails or find blog posts and tweets where people sing the praises of the products and people they've discovered through Supermarket."

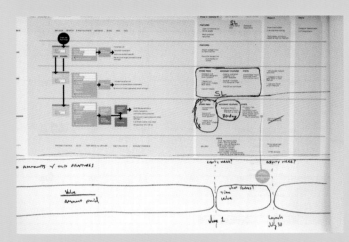
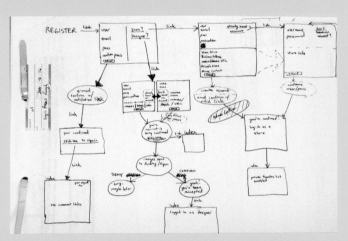
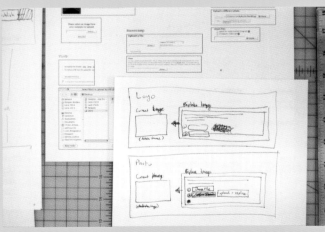

OPPOSITE
Sketches show the development of the Supermarket logo. The Supermarket audience is adults who value quality and authenticity in the products they buy. Products are purchased directly from the designers who create them.

ABOVE
The Supermarket user experience is outlined in a series of preliminary site map sketches.

Design Research Is About Better Design Thinking

Of all the design disciplines, graphic and communications design are routinely criticized for a lack of research rigor. Justifiably so, but maybe it isn't the designer's fault. Graphic designers complain that because their work is part of a holistic suite of branding activities, and there are so many different conditions and contributions to the success of branding, their work is hard to validate or measure directly. Therefore, most graphic design is considered a success because of consensus, not empirical data.

If a designer has studied the people who are being communicated with, they can better tailor their efforts to the audience's needs and preferences. Knowing people is what helps designers find those tiny inspirations that become significant insights later on in the process of creating distinct and innovative design solutions. It just makes sense to understand as much as you can about an audience before you begin to design for them.

The Design Research Society, the multidisciplinary international society for the design research community worldwide, founded in the UK in 1966, describes communication design as both "scientific and humanistic," two very contradictory forces. Because of this, designers need to observe carefully how people behave, interpret the reasons and meaning for this behavior, and either recreate or reinvent it for their clients in order to get the desired result. Simply put, research makes designers better at what they do.

Reasons for Research Failure

Like everything else about the design process, it's essential to plan and execute the research studies properly to ensure good results. Sometimes, that's not entirely possible. In that case, failure, or less than optimum results, may be obtained that lead to mistaken analysis. Some common mistakes that lead to poor research:

- **Lack of clarity:** Figure out what information you need to know up front. Any additional information uncovered becomes a bonus.

- **Wrong subjects:** Know who the target audience is for your client. Make sure to conduct research with people who fall within this description.

- **Bad instrument:** Ask the right questions using the best research method in order to yield information that actually matters.

- **Dubious sources:** When leveraging secondary or existing research, make sure the information comes from credible, verifiable sources. Double check or filter dated or biased material.

- **Limited information:** Make sure the research is thorough and not random or insufficient to draw good conclusions. Verify data by looking at several sources of information.

Most of the time, research failure means not having done it in the first place. Of course, ignoring it either selectively or entirely once it's done is another giant cause of research failure.

Three Useful Research Tactics

When it comes to research, the instinct for most designers is to utilize, or be dominated by, the visual. Just reviewing the client's existing branding efforts is going to speak volumes to a designer. Add to this a few additional tactics, and a designer has a full arsenal of information at their disposal. Things to include:

Interviews:

Personal interviews with open-ended questions can yield great information. Moderated interviews with multiple people, like focus groups, can also be helpful, if they are not lead with prejudice toward a certain result by skewed questions. Any interviews should be recorded and reviewed later for best results.

Surveys:

Use a sample group that represents the target audience and have them answer a straightforward questionnaire, either on the telephone or via direct mail. More and more, surveys are placed online with respondents self-selecting, usually incentivized by a contest.

Observations:

Sometimes, interviews and surveys provide results that are contradicted by actual behavior. Recording people in action as they interact with a product or service, whether it is actual or prototype, will give you a more accurate look at what people really do versus what they say they do.

Defining the Audience: Demographics and Ethnography

People are complex, and figuring them out is no small task. So much of creating effective design is getting the right message to the right people in the right way. For that reason, discovering and understanding the audience is essential.

Identity, Culture, and Experience

When we think about how people can be described, so many means and measurements come to mind. However, these fall roughly into three categories: identity, culture, and experience. Identity is composed of things that relate specifically to an individual, such as a person's gender, race, age, memberships, or profession. These things are clear facts, and often compiled as statistical data. They can be obtained using demographic research. Culture is a set of factors that describe a person as existing in relation to a group of others—their traditions, nationality, social norms, and religion. These are the characteristics derived from ethnographic research. Finally, experience relates to both individual and group factors: How does a person think and feel? What are their aspirations? How do they make decisions? These qualities can be studied using psychographic research.

Demographics

Characteristics that are readily quantified can produce a fact-based profile of any person. The relevant information that can help designers:

- Gender
- Age
- Race
- Ethnicity
- Education level
- Marital status
- Family size
- Income level
- Number of earners in the household
- Employment status
- Own or rent home
- Amount spent on this product/service category
- Frequency of use/purchase of this product/service

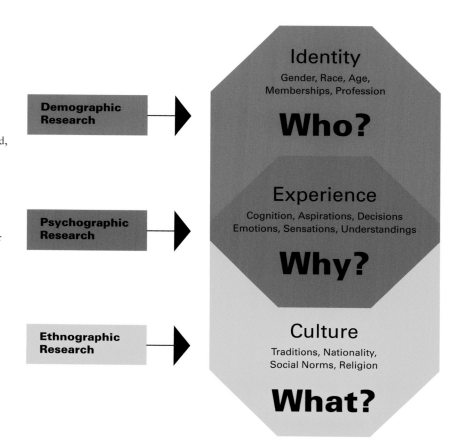

Demographic Research →

Identity
Gender, Race, Age, Memberships, Profession

Who?

Psychographic Research →

Experience
Cognition, Aspirations, Decisions Emotions, Sensations, Understandings

Why?

Ethnographic Research →

Culture
Traditions, Nationality, Social Norms, Religion

What?

Ethnographic Research Process

Ethnography

Sometimes called "field studies" or "case reports," ethnographic studies are holistic since they look at people in their natural environment, not in a laboratory.

For the most part, ethnographic research is done as direct, first-hand observation of daily behavior. Anthropologists and sociologists conduct this kind of research regularly. Increasingly, designers are participating in ethnography as part of their practice as well. The American Institute of Graphic Arts (AIGA) partnered with Cheskin, a California-based consulting firm to develop the 2008 AIGA report called *An Ethnography Primer*. (The chart, left, is adapted from the process steps outlined in this report.) Designers are encouraged to adopt this research method as a professional service or complement to their own offerings. Some designers even call this style of research "design-based research."

Ethnography dissects a person's culture and what he believes and values. What are the clues, gestures, and language he uses to interact and communicate with others? What is the ethos of this culture? When this data is translated to design, it answers the question: What is the world view and how does it influence, and dictate the thoughts and behaviors of people within the client's target audience?

To do ethnographic research well requires having patience, being unobtrusively observant, and meticulously recording what is seen. The resulting information garnered must be scrutinized and analyzed precisely to make meaningful connections and insights. At its best, ethnography reveals opportunities and nascent trends and lets designers see how the target audience views itself.

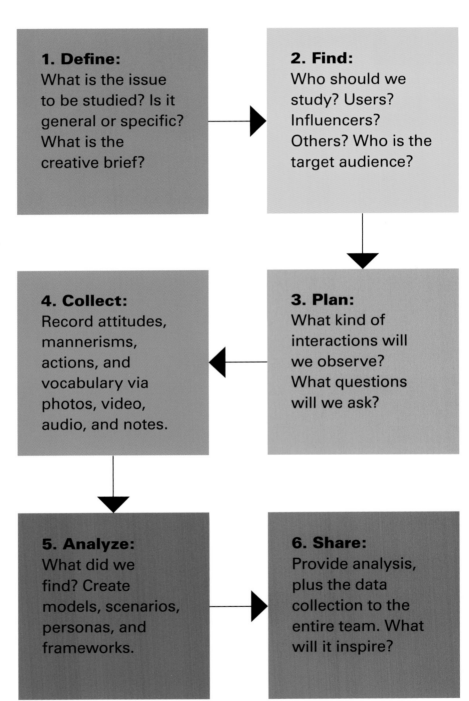

1. Define: What is the issue to be studied? Is it general or specific? What is the creative brief?

2. Find: Who should we study? Users? Influencers? Others? Who is the target audience?

3. Plan: What kind of interactions will we observe? What questions will we ask?

4. Collect: Record attitudes, mannerisms, actions, and vocabulary via photos, video, audio, and notes.

5. Analyze: What did we find? Create models, scenarios, personas, and frameworks.

6. Share: Provide analysis, plus the data collection to the entire team. What will it inspire?

Defining the Audience: Psychographics

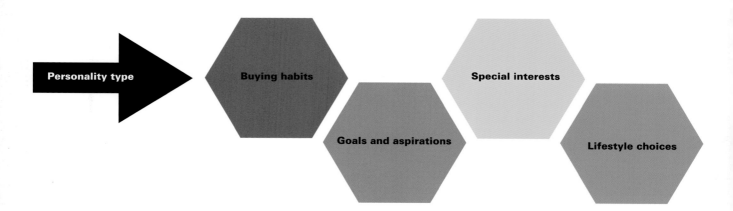

Another way to define an audience is through Psychographic Research. Psychographics explores factors that deal with a person's motivations—the "whys?" of behavior. The kind of information researched:
Personality type

▶ Buying habits
▶ Goals and aspirations
▶ Special interests
▶ Lifestyle choices

The research is obtained and is looked at using a variety of methods, including formal surveys and questionnaires, virtual and/or actual live focus groups, and software that captures customer data and matches it against consumer types and groups.

Advantages of Using Psychographics:
• Helps address the emotional factors that motivate customers
• Classifies customers according to some combination of these variables: activities, interests, and opinions
• Assists in understanding which attributes of a product or service resonate with customers
• Shows customers' predisposition toward purchasing the product or service

Disadvantages of Using Psychographics:
• Can be expensive to do a proper survey
• Target audiences for some products or services may come from a cross section of psychographic profiles, so several groups may need to be studied
• Critics complain that these studies are complicated and lack proper theoretical underpinning

VALS: Values and Lifestyle Categories
Using psychographics helps determine what type of person is most likely to respond to a client's product or service. A good study will show who these people are, as well as their needs and preferences. The Stanford Research Institute (SRI) has developed a psychographic categorization system called VALS (for "Values and Lifestyles") that breaks people into eight different clearly defined types are shown on the opposite page.

1. Innovators

- Successful with many resources
- Open to change and love variety
- Receptive to new ideas, technology, techniques
- Active consumers
- Cultured taste for upscale niche products and services

2. Thinkers

- Satisfied, reflective, motivated by ideals
- Comfortable, and well educated
- Mature reflective people who value order, knowledge, responsibility
- Actively seek out information in the decision-making process
- Conservative, practical consumers
- Look for durability and functionality

3. Achievers

- Career oriented
- Avoid risk, and value consensus, predictability, stability
- Lead conventional lives, go for the status quo
- Politically conservative and respect authority
- Active consumers
- Image is important, favor prestigious brands that demonstrate success to peers

4. Experiencers

- Impulsive, young, offbeat
- Enthusiastic, risk-takers
- Avid consumers
- Spend a comparatively high proportion of income on fashion, entertainment, socializing
- Emphasize looking good and having "cool" stuff

Principle — Status — Action

5. Believers

- Strong principles, conservative, loyal
- Conventional people with concrete beliefs based on traditional codes like: family, religion, community and nation
- Predictable consumers
- Choose familiar products and established brands

6. Strivers

- Few resources
- Approval seeking, concerned about the opinions of others
- Trendy and fun loving
- Motivated by achievement, money defines success
- Favor stylish products that mirror those of people wealthier than themselves

7. Makers

- Action-oriented, self-sufficient, do-it-yourselfers
- Motivated by self-expression
- Live within traditional context of family
- Unimpressed by material possessions other than things that are practical or functional
- Prefer value to luxury, buy basic services and products

8. Survivors

- Bottom of the ladder economically
- Lead narrowly focused lives
- Seek immediate gratification
- Comfortable with the familiar
- Primarily concerned with safety and security
- Must focus on meeting needs rather than fulfilling desires due to limited resources
- Cautious consumers, a modest market

Developed by social psychologist Kurt Lewin, the VALs Psychographic categories is a profiling system used to determine why people act the way they do.

Defining the Medium

If research is all about helping to understand how to get the right message to the right people in the right way, then a designer must use research to inform their recommendations about media as well. The best choice for one client in a certain situation may be totally wrong for another client, or even the same client when addressing another situation. For example, a direct-mail campaign to solicit funds for a nonprofit organization may have outstanding results when targeted to mature adults, but it may fail to connect with young audiences who would rather be reached via an email blast.

Design schools have evolved designer training along with changes in the graphic design profession—changes primarily driven by technological advances. Designers are trained in an approach or way of thinking that is delivery media independent. Designers who have been practicing for years know not to get too attached to any one particular means of communication. They've seen print budgets slashed, traditional advertising dissipate, and watched the rise of social media networking impact marketing tremendously. Design, in terms of delivery media, is always in a state of flux. The only constant is change.

Audience Driven

What matters most when it comes to researching and evaluating media is the audience:

- What do they use now?
- What are they most comfortable with?
- What will make the client more appealing to them?
- How do the client's competitors talk to them?

The main choices of delivery media are either physical or screen based. Some vehicles include

- Physical Delivery Media:
  - *Print*: books, brochures, magazines, newspapers, sales literature, packages, hang tags, direct mail, stationery
  - *Environmental*: signage, building graphics, interiors, trade show booths, sets, landscape elements, exhibits, retail, kiosks (might have a screen, too)

- Screen-Based Media:
  - *On-air*: television, advertising, movies, motion graphics, animation, instructional video
  - *Online*: websites, animations, movies, games, interface, interactive, advertising, blogs, WIKIs, virtual worlds, social networking media, instructional videos

Media Agnostic

The most forward-thinking designers, especially the ones who plan a lifelong career, adopt and embrace the idea of being media agnostic—designing for any and all media. They work to understand each media, the pros and cons of designing for each one—all the while being clear on how these tools are interpreted by the target audience.

Common Denominators

The common design elements used in all media must be utilized to their fullest advantage with compensation given for the variances between media. In researching delivery media choices, it's important to look at

- Content (images and words)
- Flow of information (narrative)
- Interaction (physical or virtual)
- User's behavior (pro and con)

When in doubt, and if the client budget and schedule allow, test several media to validate your decision. Design several types of pieces in a couple of different media and put them in front of the target audience in a research study. Did we accomplish what we set out to do? Did the audience accept or reject the design? What is the best media for the message?

Delivery Medium

Every type of media has its own unique advantages and disadvantages. In this age of constant bombardment, a critical decision for the designer is which medium to use in order to serve the client's objectives, schedule, and budget. Here are a few options:

Print

Pros
- Established communication medium
- Tactile
- Allows for depth of message
- Can be personalized
- Sense of seriousness and quality

Cons
- Expensive
- Limited demographic selectivity
- Sustainability issues
- Slower manufacturing and delivery
- No sound or motion

Environmental (Out of Home)

Pros
- Broad reach and high frequency
- Twenty-four-hour exposure
- Geographic selectivity
- Localized message capabilities
- Surprise factor in a specific environment

Cons
- Not for complicated messages
- Fairly high production costs
- Longer lead time to execute buy
- Coverage can be limited
- Weather and vandalism issues

On-Air

Pros
- Allows for sound and motion
- High reach potential
- Can target by program on hundreds of channels
- Mass coverage for big brands
- Catchphrases and music can permeate pop culture
- Can show the product in action
- Flexible duration, can be 30, 40, or 60 seconds long

Cons
- Higher out-of-pocket costs
- Higher production costs
- Younger audiences no longer tune in
- Less flexibility due to longer lead time
- Uneven reach by season
- Tighter restrictions on content of spot

Online

Pros
- Ties into specific community
- Able to target by format
- Allows for sound and motion
- Information medium of choice for young audiences
- It's personal, appears to be one-to-one communication
- Short lead times for scheduling and production
- Out-of-pocket cost is low
- Viral quality of messaging

Cons
- Largely, audience must seek out information
- Often a visually cluttered space
- Fragmented audiences
- Users may be otherwise occupied while viewing
- Fairly new delivery medium, not fully quantified
- Restricted to people with computers
- Individual screen settings means lack of control

Chapter 4
Strategic Thinking

Design and Strategy

In the broadest sense, strategy is a plan for how to achieve a goal. You'll hear the word used often— referring to military, political, economic, and, of course, business plans of action. In business, strategy is what bridges the gap between policy (a plan governing action, that could be referred to as "ends") and tactics (a set of techniques, that could be referred to as "means"). George Steiner, a professor of management considered to be one of the fathers of modern business strategy, explains in his 1979 book, *Strategic Planning*, that the word "strategy" is used to refer to what a business does to counter a competitor's actual or predicted moves. To summarize Steiner's definitions of strategy:

- It is what top management does that is of great importance to the organization
- Refers to purposes and missions—the basic directional decisions of an organization
- Consists of the relevant and important actions required to realize these directions
- Answers the question, "What should our organization be doing?"
- Answers the question, "What ends do we seek and how will we achieve them?"

Some clients place a lot of value in strategic planning activities and are quite formal about it. Large organizations can't afford to manage their businesses by the seat of their pants. Small, entrepreneurial clients may be much more ad hoc about strategy, with the owners of the business more or less making things up as they go along. By and large, strategy is important to business, and therefore it's important to design.

Strategy Is About Differentiation

In a 1996 *Harvard Business Review* article, professor Michael Porter argued that competitive strategy, which is arguably one of the primary focuses of design, is "about being different." He continues, "It means deliberately choosing a different set of activities to deliver a unique mix of values." Strategy helps clients achieve a competitive advantage when they understand and leverage what is distinct about themselves. In that way, they can perform different activities than their rivals, or perform similar activities, but do it in a different way. These activities must be translated to become drivers for design as well.

Many designers intuitively adopt this philosophy of differentiation (i.e., making a product different from other similar products) when creating work for clients. They constantly ask themselves: Does this make my client stand out? Will this design work with this target audience because it catches and holds their attention? Strategy becomes the framework for their design decisions augmenting the designer's intuition.

Value Disciplines

As a business, clients will probably be oriented to one of the following basic strategies, defined as "value-disciplines" by Michael Treacy and Fred Wiersema in their 1994 book, *The Discipline of Market Leaders*. These are

1. Operational Excellence:
Driven by production efficiency, the objective is to lead in terms of price and convenience. This strategy implies world-class marketing, manufacturing, and distribution processes.

2. Customer Intimacy:
Driven by customer service, the objective is long-term customer loyalty and profitability. This strategy means staying close to customers and developing real relationships with them.

3. Produce Leadership:
Driven by being state of the art, the objective is timely commercialization of new ideas. This strategy hinges on market-focused research and development and organizational agility.

Any design strategy is going to need to sync up with the basic strategic positioning of a client's business. For example, a website for a car that competes on being the lowest-priced option is going to look different than the site created for the car that is the most expensive. Reviewing clients through this filter provides yet another way to draw conclusions about what is appropriate and effective for a particular design.

What Is Design Strategy?

Design strategy, as a field of theory and practice, is a growing discipline that refers to an integrated, holistic planning process that examines the interplay between design and business strategy. However, when most designers refer to "strategy" or "a design strategy" they are referring to the following:

▶ A plan for what to make and do for a client
▶ How to use graphic design elements to meet a client's goals
▶ A pattern of actions leading to a design solution
▶ The guiding concept behind a design
▶ How to translate brand vision into designed solutions
▶ A set of creative decisions about how to approach goals, purposes, and objectives
▶ How to position the client in their competitive landscape
▶ Narrowing the design possibilities to focus the work
▶ How to innovate using design in a contextual sense
▶ How to leverage social responsibility, cultural relevance, technology, customer needs, and other factors in a design

Project Profile in Strategic Thinking

Email marketing campaign for Cusp Conference designed by SamataMason / Chicago • Vancouver
An interview with Dave Mason, creative director, SamataMason

Q. Who is the client and what is the product?

A. It's a nightmare! SamataMason is the client. The Cusp Conference is our own project. It's a two-day conference about "the design of everything." We bring together thinkers, innovators, skeptics, believers, and explorers from the arts, sciences, technology, business, government, and design to share passions and stories. Our focus is on the power of ideas, the value of imagination, and the strength of the human spirit.

We had kicked around the idea of launching Cusp for about five years. Why do a conference? Why not? We've always loved the fact that we get to work in, and learn about, so many different industries, and with so many smart, driven people. This conference is our attempt to synthesize our own experiences into a format that can be accessed by a wider audience.

Q. What is the purpose/goal of this design? What were you trying to accomplish?

A. The goal is to inform, promote, convey the essence of, and facilitate registration to the conference.

Q. What was the primary message you needed to convey? How do the design elements work to do this?

A. Primary message? That this conference will be unique, eclectic, thought provoking, entertaining, informative, surprising, and inspiring. There are other conferences, but Cusp has a broad focus on design without being narrow-minded, i.e., it's not another graphic design conference. Cusp is for T-shaped people. As far as the design elements—images, text, graphical interface—and the way they are presented, hopefully, they convey a little of that.

Q. Why does the design look the way it does? Why did you make these particular aesthetic choices?

A. It's simple, but somewhat complex. It's orderly, but surprising. That hopefully describes both the conference itself, and the design. A prominent feature is the use of enigmatic, textured images, many of which were shot by me using my iPhone. Everything about the design was selected because it seemed to feel right for the subject matter, the brand, and the audience we are hoping to reach.

Q. Why did you use e-blasts to promote the conference? I'm assuming it was partially a money issue, but other considerations?

A. Obviously cost was a factor, but also ease, flexibility, and speed. It's easier to bring the website to the people than to bring the people to the website.

Q. Did you buy lists or had you accrued tons and tons of designer's emails?

A. We had a base of contacts acquired over the years, but the list has grown considerably as a result of opt-in participation.

Q. Did you do any direct mail?

A. We did not do any direct mail. We did some online advertising through a number of sources such as media sponsors *Good* and *Communication Arts* magazines that generated solid results.

Q. In the conference's second year, you are using Twitter to promote Cusp. I don't exactly know what to make of Twitter.

A. I'm not entirely sure about Twitter either, but it seems to make sense on some levels. These people who follow 6,000 other people either know something I don't about how to process, filter, and make sense of massive amounts of unstructured data (that's the high-falutin' term we use to describe written text) or they're just insane. We haven't gone to Facebook. We can only deal with so much social media!

Q. Why do you think your target audience responded so well to your strategy?

A. I like to think first and foremost that the conference itself was interesting. The email strategy was really just the line of least resistance to connect people with it and to enable us to expand our reach exponentially.

ABOVE

A series of email newsletters inform and entice potential conference attendees. The consistent use of a black background and intriguingly obscured photography are used throughout all aspects of the Cusp branding initiatives.

It is the strategic use of delivery media (email) coupled with the graphic design (simple, yet surprising) that works effectively to appeal to Cusp's target audience of designers, scientists, and technologists.

Design as Strategic Business Tool

Both business and design strategy are about planning to meet goals, whatever they may be. All strategy needs to be sensitive and responsive to changes in the marketplace, trends, and industry/category influences. When the client is able to articulate their business strategy and that is coupled with market and consumer research, the designer has a great advantage in developing a design strategy, and executing work based on it, that will be successful. Design informed in this manner is more than window dressing or mere aesthetic modeling. It takes its place as a strategic business tool.

What's in a Design Strategy

Any design strategy should address the following:
- Opportunities to differentiate
- Unmet client/customer needs
- Existing problems
- Emerging ideas and trends

The way these issues are addressed is the essence of the strategy. When this is translated from business language and actions into design language and actions it becomes the basis for a design strategy. For example, an existing business problem may be that the client has limited product distribution. A design strategy to respond to this problem could be to set up, or it could enhance an existing e-commerce store on the client's website in order to make it more appealing for customers to buy directly from the client. In this way, design works as a strategic and a business tool.

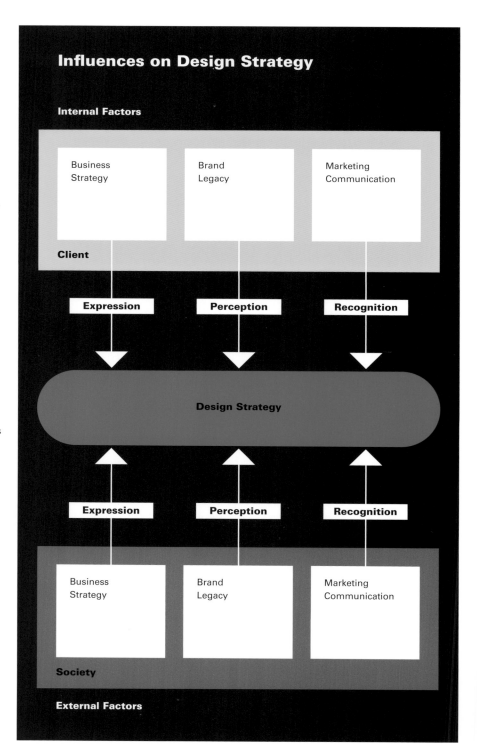

Influences on Design Strategy

Internal Factors

Business Strategy · Brand Legacy · Marketing Communication

Client

Expression · Perception · Recognition

Design Strategy

Expression · Perception · Recognition

Business Strategy · Brand Legacy · Marketing Communication

Society

External Factors

Developing a Design Strategy

Creating, implementing, and maintaining a design strategy takes a clear plan that must be evaluated and adjusted as it is evolved. The process (see chart, left) by which a design strategy is developed is logical and progresses from an initial review of goals and objectives, and continues on to a scan of the factors impacting the design. Given these things, a designer forms an action plan to meet the challenges presented to them. They then implement the design within the client's parameters, such as budget, staffing limits, and media preferences. The design strategy should be reviewed to determine if it worked as it was intended to do. It should be refined as needed, and then maintained—applying the strategy to other client projects if applicable. Design strategy is only effective if both the client and the designer are committed to its integrity.

Not having a cohesive design strategy means creating reactive, not proactive, work—hastily developed designs that meet only the immediate needs of the client, with no thought of the future. This results in a lack of a unified visual brand presence for the client over time. There is no building upon what is learned. Things are not coordinated. Because of haphazard, rather than cohesive, strategic thinking, there are fewer measurable results that would prove a design's value as well as its return on investment.

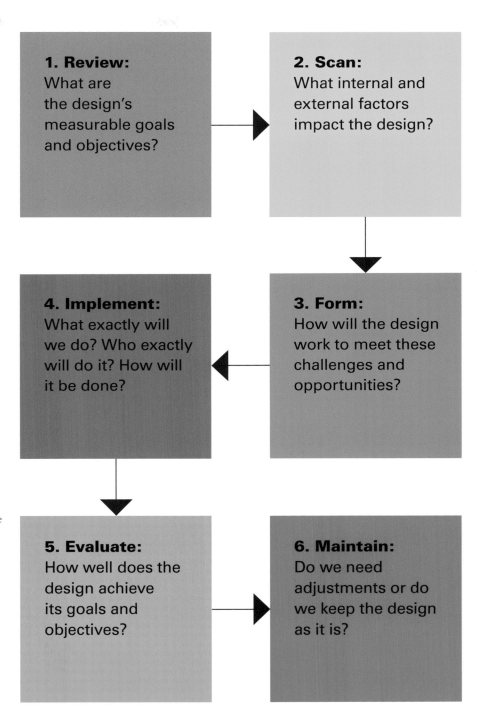

1. Review:
What are
the design's
measurable goals
and objectives?

2. Scan:
What internal and
external factors
impact the design?

3. Form:
How will the design
work to meet these
challenges and
opportunities?

4. Implement:
What exactly will
we do? Who exactly
will do it? How will
it be done?

5. Evaluate:
How well does the
design achieve
its goals and
objectives?

6. Maintain:
Do we need
adjustments or do
we keep the design
as it is?

Case Study in Strategic Thinking

Finn Creative / Kununurra, Australia

Creative director Kevin Finn likes simple design that accommodates multiple interpretations of the core ideas being expressed. Irish-born, Finn has worked in Dublin, New Zealand, and Australia, with some of the top design studios in those countries, including a stint as joint creative director of Saatchi Design, Sydney. His firm, Finn Creative is now based in Kununurra, which is a remote town in north Western Australia. There, Finn does advertising, design, photography, and branding for businesses and organizations, including local Aboriginal communities.

Wunan

Wunan is an organization that provides a diverse variety of Aboriginal programs, including work-readiness, job creation, housing, business services, construction, and maintenance. People were more familiar with Wunan's programs, than the organization itself. "It was a classic case of the 'parent brand' taking a back seat to their product/ service," notes creative director, Kevin Finn. "In some cases, this made it hard to get

funding but it also meant that Wunan had little brand awareness and not much brand equity as a result. The decision was made to centralize all departments and services under the one parent brand Wunan, and rebrand the organization."

"One of the core messages of Wunan is the desire to support equality, which is something I am sad to say is still not afforded to the majority of Aboriginal people," explains Finn. "I felt that, if equality is part of the vision, perhaps Wunan should wear their heart on their sleeve and use the rebranding project to present a statement of intent based on equality." The idea is literally shown in the Wunan logo with the mathematical symbol for "equals." In addition, Finn rejected using cliché visuals commonly employed to represent Aboriginal culture, like dot paintings and boomerangs, in favor of a bold, professional presentation.

BELOW
In developing the identity, Finn was tasked with selecting a typeface to capture Aboriginal culture. "I needed to find a font that could possibly portray the landscape that Aboriginal people associate with," says Finn, "as well perhaps *reflecting* (rather than defining) their culture, which is historically nomadic and continues to be challenged by today's mainstream society that is slowly eroding Aboriginal culture. Resisting the temptation to define an evolving culture, I felt the font Blur went some way toward representing the changes within Aboriginal culture, which are still finding shape, as well as conveying the shimmering tropical heat."

wunan ⊜ Aboriginal people succeeding through ability, opportunity and reward for effort.

Gelganyem Trust

Gelganyem Trust, is an Aboriginal trust Group set up to manage the royalty payments from Argyle Diamond Mine to the Aboriginal Traditional Owners on whose land they mine. The objective was to present the past, present, and future relationship (and agreements) between the communities and the mining company. In addition, the design needed to appeal to the corporate sector without alienating the Aboriginal communities. Finn's approach was to find the common ground between two vastly different groups, which turned out to be, quite literally, the ground. "What might appear to some people as a simple pile of dirt on the brochure cover has incredible economic significance for the resources sector and enormous cultural significance for the Aboriginal communities," Finn explains. "With this being the common factor, the rest of the design material simply used the red earth to generate a visual language that can be appreciated and understood by all involved."

OPPOSITE AND LEFT
Finn again eschews the use
of visual clichés to represent
Aboriginal peoples. "Use
of Aboriginal visual cues, like
dot paintings and boomerangs,
are employed by designers
who have no understanding of
their cultural or geographical
significance," he says.

"The design approach was
based on a simple question:
If the content is about the land,
why not use the land?" explains
creative director Kevin Finn.

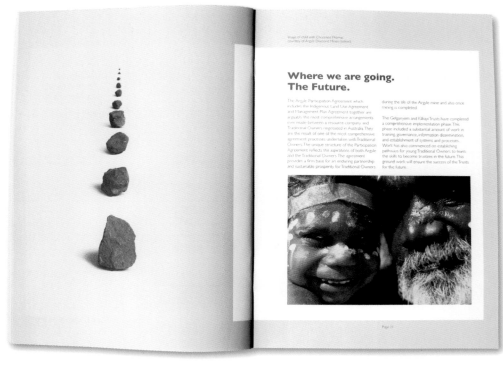

Where we are going.
The Future.

The Argyle Participation Agreement which includes the Indigenous Land Use Agreement and Management Plan Agreement together are arguably the most comprehensive arrangements ever made between a resource company and Traditional Owners negotiated in Australia. They are the result of one of the most comprehensive agreement processes undertaken with Traditional Owners. The unique structure of the Participation Agreement reflects the aspirations of both Argyle and the Traditional Owners. The agreement provides a firm basis for an enduring partnership and sustainable prosperity for Traditional Owners during the life of the Argyle mine and also once mining is completed.

The Gelganyem and Kilkayi Trusts have completed a comprehensive implementation phase. This phase included a substantial amount of work in training, governance, information dissemination and establishment of systems and processes. Work has also commenced on establishing pathways for young Traditional Owners to learn the skills to become trustees in the future. This ground work will ensure the success of the Trusts for the future.

Wizard of Oz

This poster was designed as part of an
Australian national poster competition. It was
an open brief to respond to the theme that
year—two lines from the Australian National
Anthem: "Our land abounds in Nature's gifts,
of beauty rich and rare." Finn's approach was
to present a visual comment on the apparent
disproportionate influence America had at
the time on Australian foreign policy, and to
ask whether this was a good thing. "The title
of the poster is also two-fold: 'The Wizard of
Oz' refers to Australia (Oz) but also to 'the
man behind the curtain pulling the strings,' in
this case, it was America pulling the stings on
Australia," Finn explains. The poster was one
of fifty selected for exhibition in Melbourne,
Australia, then it went on as one of twelve
exhibited in Stockholm.

Form Gallery: Canning Stock Route

Form Gallery sought to celebrate the famous Canning Stock Route of Western Australia and the nine Aboriginal communities that are associated with the route. To increase funding and to seek out new funding partners, Form Gallery decided to produce an eighty-eight-page prospectus outlining the progress, and the plans for the project. The target audience was predominantly the resources sector, many of whom have mines in the area around the Canning Stock Route. In this project, Finn does use an Aboriginal dot painting as imagery. "It serves a number of purposes: the first, to highlight the Aboriginal nature of the project; the second, to utilize the texture of the image to represent the land along the route; and the third, to leverage the dots in the painting to represent the physical track of the Canning Stock Route and the 'wells' that mark the route," Finn notes. "The decision was made by the client not to include any text on the cover, something I wholeheartedly supported. The painting wraps around to the back cover, which provides a stunning visual."

BELOW
Art, like the paintings used in this brochure, is a key ritual of great significance in Aboriginal culture. It is often used to tell sacred stories, mark community territories, and record ancestral history.

NEXT SPREAD
Interior pages from the prospectus reflect the rich culture of Australia's Aboriginal communities.

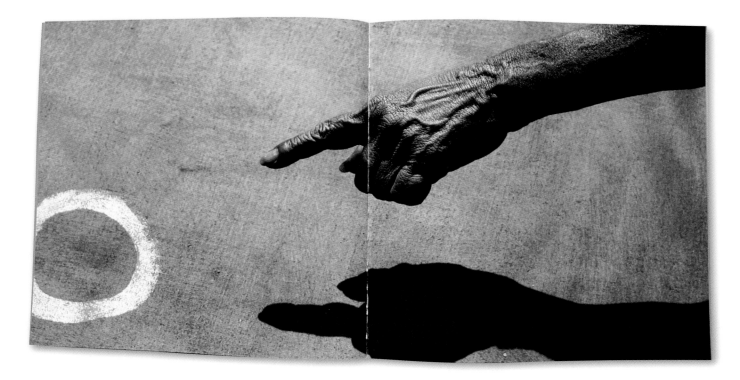

Opposite page:
Droving cattle along the
CSR, detail of a triptych
by Mervyn Street from
Mangkaja Arts.
Watercolour on paper.

Page 33

…*The white man history has been told and it's today in the book. But our history is not there properly. That's one way to tell 'em. We've got to tell 'em through our paintings. They might see it through there.*

Clifford Brooks, Martu, Tjukurba Gallery.

The Canning Stock Route Project is evolving a model for ongoing art centre partnerships and enterprise – a touchstone for the artists involved – with benefits channeled directly back into communities. It is unfolding into:
- A world class exhibition of paintings, photographs, 3-dimensional cultural artefacts and new media presentations;
- A major publication;
- Short films by Aboriginal and non-Aboriginal filmmakers.

The Canning Stock Route Project has established a strong collaboration among nine Aboriginal arts centres, cultural organisations and their communities, which will help to build social capital in some of the most remote environments of Australia.

Warlayirti Artists, Balgo.
Paraku IPA, Mulan.
Ngurra Artists, Wangkajunga.
Mangkaja Arts, Fitzroy Crossing.
Yulparija Artists, Bidyadanga.
Martumili Artists, Newman.
Papunya Tula Artists, Kiwirrkurra.
Kayili Artists, Patjarr.
Tjukurba Gallery, Wiluna.

Opposite page
Eubena Nampitjin from
Warlayirti Artists.

...Canning Stock Routeparnatju ngurra wakaninpa.

Eubena Nampitjin, Kukatja, Warlayirti Artists

...That's what I'm painting, my Country, the Canning Stock Route.

Managing Aesthetic Strategy

Whether you are a designer or their client, you'll eventually need to review, analyze, and evaluate the appropriateness of any design solution in light of the objectives identified for the project. Determining if the design will support your goals and appeal to your audience are the essential metrics. Beyond the typical, "Do I like it?" or "Does it work?" are some open-ended more powerful questions to ask:

	Yes	No
Is it authentic?		
Is it credible?		
Is it accurate?		
Is the hierarchy of the elements correct?		
Does it reflect the client's unique personality?		
Is it on message?		
Is it innovative?		
Is it interesting?		
Is it compelling?		
Does it have emotional impact?		
Is it provocative?		
Does it invite interaction?		
How does it compare to competitors?		
Is it different (or similar) enough?		
Is it an unexpected solution for us? Is that good or bad?		
Will it stand out in the environment it needs to?		
Does it take a risk or play it safe?		
Can we implement it within the project parameters?		
Is anything unsatisfactory? What specifically? Why?		

Project Profile in Strategic Thinking

Les Allusifs designed by Paprika / Montreal, Canada

Editions Les Allusifs is a small publishing house that translates internationally renowned fiction and nonfiction books into French and distributes them to French-speaking countries around the globe. Their books are often intellectually and artistically challenging works, which tend to distinguish them from larger more commercially oriented publishing companies. One of the key missions for *Les Allusifs* (which translates to *the Allusives*) is to provide books that appeal to readers, tied together by a common language, but representing a variety of cultures. The publisher chose Montreal design firm, Paprika, to help accomplish this goal through design, working together over the course of several years. Paprika was recently challenged to create a lighter mood

and more lively presence for the *Les Allusifs* products. "We decided to use different colors to refresh the look, while making sure that these new additions would still fit with previously published works," says Louis Gagnon, Paprika creative director. Another important decision was to collaborate, since the beginning, with illustrator Alain Pilon, for all of the distinctive cover illustrations. "Our work always 'depends' on the illustration, which itself 'depends' on the text of the book. So everything has to be coherent together," explains Gagnon. This harmony is especially apparent in the series of novels by Tecia Werbowski. "Each of *Les Allusifs*' books is unique, and as a collection, they now have a great unity and a major impact on the shelves of bookstores," says Gagnon.

BELOW AND OPPOSITE
Paprika presented several concepts of a general design layout template for this collection of novels. One of these mockups presented to the client was prepared with an existing illustration by Alain Pilon. That was the concept that the client selected, and as a result, the book covers were illustrated by Pilon. All of the *Les Allusifs* book covers feature a strong bold graphic sensibility. The title set in a simple sans serif font encapsulated with a circle acts as a unifying element.

The *Les Allusif* Concept Development Process

- The client supplied the designers with a synopsis of every book to be published.
- The designers went through those documents, then discussed with the illustrator which aspects of the stories should be focused on.
- The illustrator worked on sketches and sent them to the designers for review and comment.
- The designers selected the direction they wanted to recommend to client, and after some refinement, the designers prepared a mock-up for the client with color background, illustration, type, etc.
- The client occasionally made some changes, or simply approved the work and ordered final files for printing.

Case Study in Strategic Thinking

Good Design Company / Tokyo, Japan

Good Design Company was founded in 1999 by art director/president, Manabu Mizuno. Since then, this multidisciplined design firm, based in Ebisu, the design hub of Tokyo, has created advertising, product planning, print, books, identity, package design and interior design for a variety of Japanese and international brands. The firm also does retail and furniture design. Their work captures a contemporary, yet classic, elegance.

Potsunen Drop

The announcement for *Potsunen*, a one-person play project from the solo performer Kentaro Kobayashi. This actor, playwright, and director worked with Good Design Company to create a design that explains the nature of the project. "In order to express a slightly mysterious, unique worldview, items used in past performances were made and incorporated," explains art director/president Manabu Mizuno. "Devices were also incorporated into the visual. We thought of building the Postunen project brand by surprising fans with 'yes, they did it again this time!'"

JAGDA

The Japanese Graphic Design Association (JAGDA) is the only national graphic designer's organization in Japan. Each year, the organization recognizes excellence in the design community. When Good Design Company's art director/founder Manabu Mizuno won the JAGDA Rookie of the Year award in 2003, the firm produced this as a visual for a book that was published to commemorate the exhibition and award.

Suntory: Shinruchu

When sales of Shinruchu apricot wine declined by seventy percent compared to the previous year, Japanese brewing and distilling company, Suntory, decided to launch a television and print advertising campaign to reinvigorate sales. Good Design Company created the campaign and rebranded the drink to get rid of the negative image of "this is a liquor that was popular ten years ago but nobody drinks it now." Shinruchu was originally designed to appeal to young women as a sweet alcoholic beverage they would enjoy. "With this in mind, as a visual tone, we united them by using a soft, light pretty tone, one that would be well received by women who are oriented toward natural products," says art director/president, Manabu Mizuno. The campaign was a huge success, and increased sales immediately—140 percent over the previous year.

Kukuyo Design Awards

Office supply giant Kokuyo annually sponsors the Kokuyo Design Awards, which recognizes outstanding product design worldwide. In 2007, Good Design Company created an iconic hexagon visual to represent the awards. For the 2008 awards, the announcement poster had an "unfolding pattern" with a hexagon as the base. It is a colorful solution with a coolness about it that gives the impression that this was a high-quality award. The poster connected with its audience, increasing the number of entries.

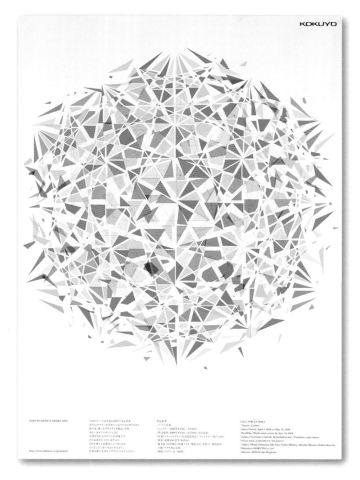

Tokyo Midtown

Tokyo Midtown, a group of various buildings such as art galleries, restaurants, and fashion shops, opened in 2007 in the Roppongi district, a popular tourist area known for its nightlife. Good Design Company produced a visual announcement notice for a design event, Midtown Design Touch 2008, being held there (top). "We didn't want it to just look lively, we created the visual thinking of the need for Tokyo Midtown to be seen as a 'town where culture is transmitted from,'" says Mizuno. "We built a visual with the motifs of 'books' which are crammed with information, and 'apples' which are the symbol of wisdom."

The invitation for a spring event at Tokyo Midtown, called "Midtown Blossomed," celebrates the development's second anniversary. The graphics emphasize the many "Sakura" cherry blossom trees that were blooming in the premises. "Because it was at a time when the world had fallen into recession, and in Japan as well the news was all bad, we wanted to give people who looked at it a cheerful feeling when they saw the visual posted throughout the building," explains Mizuno. "Another consideration of importance was the fact that for the Japanese, Sakura is a beautiful sign that spring is here, welcoming the breath of life, the awe of things beautiful, as well as the transience and sorrow of the blossoms falling. With this in mind, we didn't just focus on the cherry blossoms, we created a magical visual with young girls dancing among the falling cherry blossoms."

ITOKI

ITOKI hired Good Design Company to create an ad campaign for its line of women's office chairs. Mizuno felt that a sophisticated visual would work to build the ITOKI brand, which was number three in its industry. "Starting from keywords of 'good for your body,' and 'feeling of trust,' we came up with the red cross concept," explains Mizuno. "However, with the red cross, images of sickness and injury were too strong. With this in mind, we planned to create balance by changing it to a light emerald green cross, using delicate writing and a soft tone." The design received high praise, and was linked to increased sales.

Laforet Harajuku

Laforet Harajuku, the department store and museum where cutting-edge original fashion has been dispatched for over thirty years, is a landmark of the Harajuku area of Tokyo. It is a place known as a hub for youth culture and radical street fashion. Good Design Company was commissioned to create a party invitation for Laforet. In order to get noticed, the designers decided to make a poster mailed in a large semi-transparent envelope with the word *invitation* and the date printed in large letters. From close up it looks just like a colorful dot pattern, but if you look at it from a little further away, a skull and crossbones pattern emerges. "We expressed both the fun and flashiness of fashion and Laforet Harajuku's edginess," explains Manabu Mizuno.

Laforet Private Party

Project Profile in Strategic Thinking: Saatchi & Saatchi

Olay designed by Saatchi & Saatchi / Moscow, Russia

Saatchi & Saatchi Russia is part of the Saatchi & Saatchi network of iconic global advertising agencies that has 135 offices in 85 countries. Saatchi is famous for its belief in the power of big ideas to transform their client's brands, businesses, and reputations.

Olay Total Effects

Under the creative direction of Stuart Robinson, the Moscow office designed the "Correct Your Age" campaign for Olay Total Effects. The campaign was targeted to women ages thirty-five to forty-five, of middle and upper-middle income, who wish to look younger and more beautiful. Using numbers and drops of cream, the executions show the product in action—visibly removing several years from age.

47

Correct your age

Evaluating Design Strategy

If the design is driven by the client's desire to achieve a measurable goal or objective, then it's pretty obvious as to whether or not the design succeeded in achieving the goal. For example, if the goal was to release a brochure in the first quarter of the year, it either happened or it didn't. Some objectives are less black and white in terms of design's responsibility in achieving them. If the objective was to shift brand perception and appeal to a slightly different audience by refreshing a product identity, chances are that many factors, beyond a new logo, impacted whether or not the shift occurred.

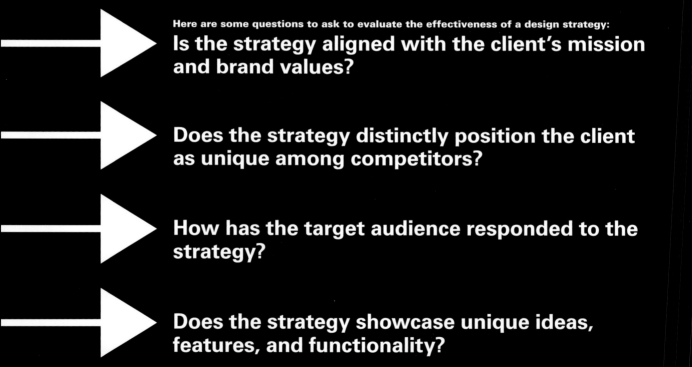

Here are some questions to ask to evaluate the effectiveness of a design strategy:

Is the strategy aligned with the client's mission and brand values?

Does the strategy distinctly position the client as unique among competitors?

How has the target audience responded to the strategy?

Does the strategy showcase unique ideas, features, and functionality?

Has the strategy garnered industry attention?

Articulating Design Strategy

Like every other aspect of the design process, at some point, a design strategy must be clearly articulated to the client. They need to understand the rationale and the design decisions within a business context. Good clients expect their designer to be an artist working within business environments, but they need to understand design as something more than an arbitrary creative endeavor.

Since design strategy is the underlying game plan for all subsequent work a designer will do, it is worth taking the time to present it well. Using concise language and a well-designed PDF, booklet, or slide show, will help clients visualize the strategy much more easily. If they understand it, and it is well formulated and articulated, the client is much more likely to approve it.

The key to successfully presenting a design strategy is in helping clients form an image in their mind that seems actionable. They can see how the design will become a tangible tool to help them achieve their goals. Plus, they will more easily be able to articulate the strategy to others, which is important, because a designer's client contact must often sell the design strategy to their own internal team members. Providing your client contact person with the tools and information they need to do this well is a great way to insure their success.

With the approval of the design strategy, the designer has taken a critical step toward making sure that what they design for the client will be well received and approved throughout the design process from ideation to completion.

Project Profile in Strategic Thinking

UCLA Anderson School of Management designed by AdamsMorioka, Inc. / Beverly Hills, California • New York, New York USA

With offices in Beverly Hills, California, and New York City, AdamsMorioka's work ranges from corporate identities, identity systems, print campaigns, and environmental graphics to motion and digital projects, animation, and websites.

UCLA Anderson School of Management

The Anderson School of Management at University of California, Los Angeles (UCLA) offers graduate degrees and MBAs in business management. AdamsMorioka rebranded the UCLA Anderson School's Executive Education, a program that offers intensive certificate programs for business executives and managers. Each year, more than forty programs are offered that incorporate the most recent innovations in management education. Creating a compelling identity and suite of marketing materials that capture the essence of the client's forward-thinking culture was the designers' objective.

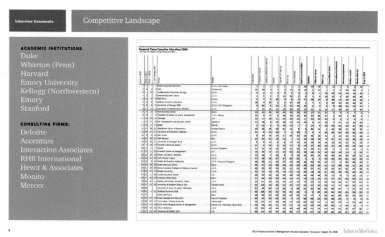

RIGHT
AdamsMorioka created a visually appealing document that outlined their design thinking. Each page of the document steps the client through the strategy and design criteria.

ADAPT. CATALYZE. TRANSFORM.

EXECUTIVE EDUCATION

UCLAAnderson
School of Management

Common Mistakes in Design Strategy

Developing, articulating, and implementing a successful design strategy is a complex task. It's an exciting challenge for any designer to get it just right. Of course, sometimes even the best-laid plans go awry. Here are some things to watch out for:

- ▶ Lack of participation from the client
- ▶ Rushed or haphazard backgrounding
- ▶ Insufficient thinking and analysis
- ▶ Simplistic reactions to complicated issues
- ▶ Inability to make decisions
- ▶ Lack of focus on specific details
- ▶ Overly elaborate plans that go nowhere
- ▶ No buy-in from key individuals
- ▶ Lack of oversight and commitment
- ▶ Piecemeal instead of holistic approach
- ▶ Pessimism or intimidation
- ▶ Lack of drive or passion
- ▶ Attachment to the status quo
- ▶ Murky communications
- ▶ Fear of the unknown or untried
- ▶ People just don't like it

Like the old saying goes, "Forewarned is forearmed." If a designer knows that these things can torpedo a design strategy before it even has a chance to be acted upon, then they can take steps to guard against these negative and limiting problems.

Project Profile in Strategic Thinking: Marco Morosini

Mister Nut designed by Marco Morosini Studio / Pesaro, Italy

Mister Nut

Marco Morosini Studio is lead by creative director Marco Morosini, an alumnus of Oliviero Toscani's Fabrica, the studio responsible for the indelible images at Bennetton in the early 1990s. Since then, he has taught, authored several books, had his artwork exhibited around the world, launched his own products, and opened his studio, which focuses on branding.

For the snack food brand, Mister Nut, the studio created a packaging system aimed at enhancing the reputation of the product, particularly with organic food lovers. This has resulted in packaging that exalts the concept of transparency, purity, and simplicity. An extremely important feature is the innovative material used; it is 100 percent biodegradable and, thus, fully respects the environment.

OPPOSITE AND BELOW
"Our aim is to reduce the environmental impact by using Nature-Flex NK by Innovia Films U.K., a high-barrier, compostable, transparent film derived from renewable sources," says Morosini. "Goodness and healthiness at a glance."

Chapter 5
Informed Risk Taking

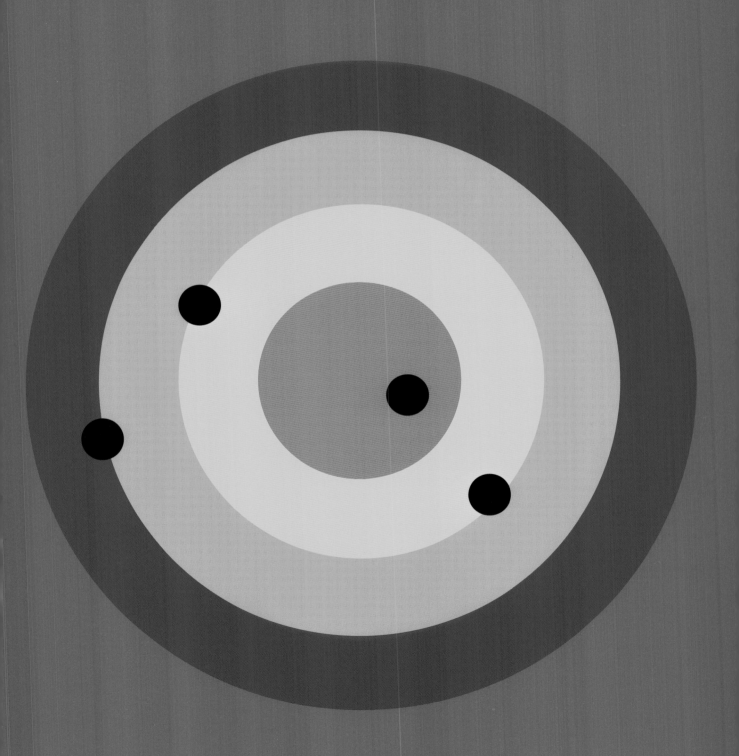

Taking Creative Risks

There is a lot of competition in a client's world—whether they are working to differentiate their existing product from competitor's or simply trying to get noticed in the first place. Winning in the face of competition means standing out. That often means daring to be different. It means taking creative risks and pushing the design.

For any given assignment, a good designer will typically explore a range of solutions from mild to wild. They'll often present a client with design options that are well within the comfort zone but provide what is, in essence, a refresh of an existing design system of graphic elements. These designs are safe.

On the opposite end of the spectrum, more daring designers will show unexpected and intriguing concepts that confront preconceived notions. The client is faced with an interesting dilemma—go with safe and expected or take a chance on the innovative and unusual. For some, it's a clear-cut decision. Other clients become completely uncertain about which direction to move in. This situation often leads to clients cherry-picking different aspects of the design that they like, while diluting others in an attempt to mitigate uncertainty. This compromised "Frankenstein" approach usually results in ineffective designs that please nobody.

Here's where that degree in psychology would come in handy...

Encouraging Risky Design

So how do you get a client to take a leap of faith, trust the designer's expertise, and take a creative risk? By being respectful, methodical, and professional. "Risky" implies something negative to many clients. It might mean danger, tension, or even loss. Those are the people who see only the down side of risk, not its potential upside benefits of being truly innovative. Risk does involve some gambling. In design, risk is about developing work that sets a new standard, while still meeting stated client goals. New is unusual, and new can be scary.

Making informed and calculated creative risks means limiting negative outcomes as much as possible. The way to accomplish this is to have clear goals and objectives, be very aware of the audience, understand what the competition is doing, know where the client fits into the picture, and be sure of what must be communicated. In short, do the background set-up work that is so essential to design. Then evaluate the design solutions, risky or not, against that criteria.

Assessing Risk

The decision to take a creative risk or play it safe depends on many factors:

How big is the client organization?

Large companies move slowly, are often risk-averse, and typically have layers of management for a designer to wade through. Small organizations can compete by being nimble and bold, and designers frequently work directly with the owner/CEO. These are generalizations, but more often than not, they hold true.

How high profile is the project?

Challenging design for small initiatives, seen by limited audiences, like the client's annual employee picnic invitation, are easier to approve than large-scale projects seen by many, such as the redesign of the client's identity.

How fierce is the competition?

If the client is being beaten in the marketplace by aggressive or more effective competitors, then he may be willing to take a chance. If, however, his company is seated in the top spot, he may not want to rock the boat.

What is the product/ service category?

The public expects some industries to be cautious, solid, even conservative, such as medical and financial companies. Other businesses and organizations are trend driven or cutting edge, such as technology, fashion, athletics, and the arts.

What is the client culture like?

As a group, and as a brand, are they dynamic and flexible or are they drawn to safety and security?

Who is the client contact?

Sometimes, it all comes down to the personality of whoever represents the client. Are they adventurous or part of the status quo?

Project Profile in Informed Risk Thinking

Currency magazine designed by Change Is Good / Paris

Change Is Good is the Paris-based design duo of José Albergaria, who is Portuguese, and Rik Bas Backer, who is Dutch. They focus on spontaneity, provocation, and always take chances in their design. Many of their clients are artists and cultural institutions who appreciate risky choices. *Currency* magazine, published and co–art directed by internationally recognized artist Sico Carlier, is an example of this. Although the publication contains traditional magazine content like photography, drawings, essays, and interviews, both contemporary and previously published material as old as twenty-five years, the structure is anything but conventional.

To start, there is the hard cover, inspired by the *Les Aventures de Tintin* Belgian comic strip books, giving the appearance of a hybrid book/magazine. "The other 'risky' element is that the grid is very complex and does not respect a usual continuation," explains Albergaria. "It's like a labyrinth—the text follows on the same column of the page, from page to page, and not from column to column!" All of which makes the text, which is written in French, English, and German, an intriguing art puzzle to experience.

BELOW

Currency has a simple grid, used in a way that troubles reading on purpose. Text starts in one column in a spread and then flows to the next double-page spread, not the adjacent column, as expected. There can be up to eight different texts simultaneously on a spread. It is a design solution chosen to confront subjects and iconography by placing them in parallel with each other. New connections are formed, and conventional ideas are challenged. Japanese art director/designer, Hideki Nakajima, has said of *Currency*, "It's pretty confusing in an amusing way. I believe this is an act of a self-assured criminal."

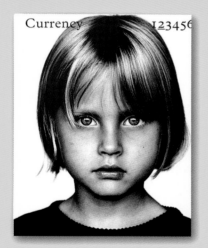

ABOVE
The *Currency* magazine cover.

Risk versus Uncertainty

Doing something different can cause uncertainty. It's human nature. The truth is, we are never sure exactly how an audience will or won't connect with a particular design. We can take the fear out and make an informed decision by assessing these variables: Can we afford to stay static and do only an incremental design change or not? Are we more or less vulnerable if we change radically?

Mostly, we are faced with uncertainty because a design is so subjectively processed by each person who experiences it. In the financial world, people understand the relationship between risk and reward. Riskier opportunities often mean greater return on investment. This is not always true in design. Sometimes, it is the safe solution that is most appropriate. It all comes down to the skill of the client in framing the design problem and the knowledge and expertise of the designer who is solving it. Essentially, uncertainty is an ongoing factor in graphic design. At some point, it all comes down to trust.

Building Courage

It might make some clients less apprehensive if you can define what is acceptable risk and what is unacceptable. For example, is it going too far to violate an established corporate identity system? Can the rules be bent? Can new rules be added? It's best to know at the beginning of a design project.

Some ways to make creative risk-taking less risky:

▶ Be consistent with the essence of the client's brand.

▶ Be authentic. If it's not true, the design is a lie.

▶ Amplify the client's strengths. Address weaknesses in the design thinking.

▶ Differentiate by emphasizing what makes the brand unique.

▶ Recontextualize the client's business category by considering their customers' total lifestyle.

▶ Do involve the client's customers. Listen to them.

▶ Don't play to the lowest common denominator, take it up to a higher level.

▶ Remember, "No guts, no glory."

▶ When in doubt, trust the designer's intuition.

Case Study in Informed Risk Taking

Asylum / Singapore

Asylum is a creative company engaged in a range of activities—a design studio, a retail store, a workshop, and a record label. Since its inception in 1999, Asylum has worked on cross-disciplinary projects, including interactive design, product development, environment and interior design, packaging, apparel design, branding, and graphic design.

Creative director Chris Lee and his team have a taste for the experimental—whether it is in their commercial work or their own self-initiated projects. "I'm always keen on blurring the lines between disciplines because the results are always more exciting. Fusing art and commercial design allows us to create the content instead of just crafting it."

Times of Jakarta

Times bookstores are a chain of retail outlets throughout Singapore, Indonesia, Macau, and Malaysia that offer readers of all ages and interests a wide variety of books. Times also hosts events, including author appearances, book signings, and workshops for customers.

OPPOSITE
The center of attraction is an indoor garden that is a perfect place to relax and read.

ABOVE
"There are gigantic wall murals with laser-cut names of famous authors," says Asylum creative director Chris Lee. "If you do not like to read books but want a quick way to sound well-read, look to the walls and memorize noteworthy quotes by the likes of Mark Twain and Simone Weil."

ABOVE
Designed to be engaging and inspiring environments that are conducive to book appreciation, the Times bookstore UPH at Karawaci Village in Jakarta, Indonesia, offers 13,000 square feet (1,209 m²) of space that revolves around the concept of "A Garden of Discovery." Book lovers can get lost and discover the over 100,000 books found on shelves arranged in meandering, mazelike patterns.

Little Village

Little Village is a child development center that provides a sensorial learning environment that is both stimulating and inviting. Drawing inspiration from the natural landscape surrounding it, Asylum created a unique identity, differentiating it from the conventional ideas about schools. It is a playful, kinetic identity system that references the way children learn through imagination and creativity. Primarily, it features a range of animals and series of pastel patterns that display a fun childlike innocence. The risk in this identity was in highlighting innocent play rather than solid educational benefits.

Utter Rubbish

As part of the Singapore Design Festival, *Utterubbish* was an exhibition held at the old Parliament House with recycling as its underlying theme. Asylum collected junk mail from mailboxes around the island and reused them as notebook covers and stationery, giving these ugly mailers a new lease of life. This self-initiated project allowed the designers to step away from their commercial work and think in new ways about the value of design. They risked the acknowledgment that graphic designers' work can be seen as garbage or as an opportunity for reinvention.

Asylum's Winning Strategy

1. Take briefs with an enthusiastic expression.
2. Smile with sincerity as you talk.
3. Buy the client lunch.
4. Quote twenty percent less than the next competitor.
5. Show 50 ideas the next day.

Chocolate Research Facility

The Chocolate Research Facility is a brand of artisan chocolates, as well as a concept boutique and café, in Singapore's Millenia Walk. The creators concocted over 100 different flavors of chocolate bar, including unconventional flavors like yam with almond to classics like hazelnut. Asylum branded and developed the design of both the packaging and the store. The overall concept takes a creative risk by eschewing traditional candy store iconography. At first glance, the Chocolate Research Facility appears to be a generic-looking research laboratory and brand. However, both the store and the chocolate bars themselves open to reveal bursts of color and flavor.

BELOW LEFT
The retail space sports clinical white interiors and a shop window containing rows of LED numbers akin to the running numbers in a laboratory. The boutique also features a café, which serves an array of chocolate delights.

BELOW AND OPPOSITE
Each bar comes in an understated monochromatic box. It is a deceptively sedate initial surface. The chocolate bars are wrapped in a fun series of pop-art patterns.

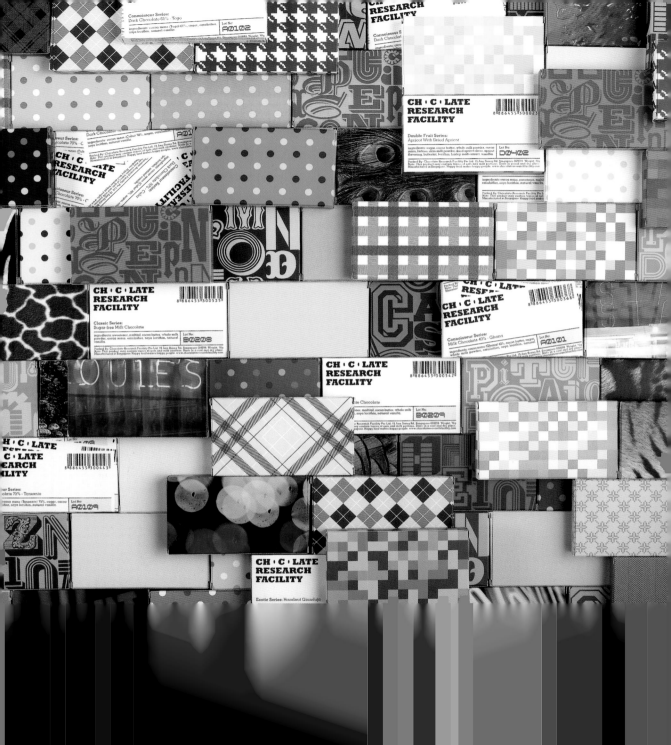

Innovative Design Means Taking a Calculated Risk

The best clients for designers are the ones who really know their company and brand inside and out. They understand who they are as an organization, know who they want to talk to about their product/service, and what they want to communicate to them. They know what they want people to do upon experiencing a design—whether it is buying a ticket to Tahiti, eating more pretzels, or going to a sporting event.

The Importance of CEO Leadership

A client who knows enough to hire a great design consultant and then let them do their job to the fullest is a treasured partner indeed. These are the kind of clients that empower, support, and then advocate for their designers. If this client also happens to be the chief executive of the organization, even better.

Designers often seem to lack a certain professional credibility, because they are perceived as "creative types" rather than highly trained experts. It's the kind of attitude that cripples their effectiveness. However, when the CEO is on board and sanctions the work, designers find themselves in a significantly better position to move confidently through projects. This is especially critical when leading a client to adopt a seemingly "risky" design solution.

Decision Making Styles

From gray-haired CEOs to inexperienced, young middle managers, and everything in between, designers deal with a wide range of personality types. Not only does the designer need to work within the comfort zone of the organizational culture, they need to interact with individuals, too. Each person can have their own decision-making style that affects how and what designs get acted upon.

There is a lot of information available about cognitive processes. Understanding how people think allows a designer to work with clients in a way that makes them most comfortable. Unfortunately, you can't give each new client a personality test at the kick-off meeting. Usually, a designer finds out through trial and error what works with each of their clients. By the end of the project, they know exactly who they are dealing with (and vice versa)

Creating Certainty

No matter what the personality, perhaps the strongest means of appeal will be a methodical mapping of the design solution's appropriateness in meeting stated objectives. Something that has a universal appeal is a conviction and enthusiasm for the new design. People respond to sureness. They may not agree with the idea, but they'll at least listen.

Presenting Risky Ideas

How can a designer elevate their clients' levels of trust in them? Truthfully, everything they have done in terms of the way they have conducted business prior to any creative being shown sets the stage for that first creative presentation. Was the designer consistent, professional, and polished? Hopefully that is the case, because when the rubber meets the road and it is presentation time—especially with unusual design solutions—it's time to win over clients. Having a well-orchestrated creative presentation is essential, too. Here are some tips on making presentations run more smoothly and be more effective:

1 Do the initial creative presentation in person. It is not always possible, but it is valuable to be able to gauge reactions and pick up on nonverbal cues.

2 Keep design rationale statements brief and the language simple. Exhaustive explanations filled with jargon mostly sound hyperbolic and insincere.

3 Maintain eye contact and don't read to them. It's a live performance meant to personally connect you and the client with each other, and to the design.

4 Make the visuals to right scale for the presentation. If it's to one person at their desk make it smaller. For a large group in a conference room, project large visuals from a laptop onto a wall—or even safer, print it out on large sheets.

5 Associate your design choices with the client's goals and objectives. Explain aesthetics only in those terms. Avoid justifications of personal preferences. Make sure the client gets that these are not arbitrary, but design solutions based on real information.

6 Be clear, respectful, and respond to client questions regarding the presentation. Don't be defensive. Listen. Address concerns. Go back and reiterate how this design works to solve their problem. If revisions are requested, summarize what is needed.

7 Don't design at the table. If revisions and refinements must be made, thank them for their input and leave the presentation with a timetable for the next presentation. Come back and do it all again.

Case Study in Informed Risk Taking

Brand New School / Los Angeles • New York

Brand New School (BNS) is a bicoastal directing collective working in all fields of commercial art. With offices in New York and Los Angeles, this ever-evolving studio cultivates a sense of wonder and exploration. They are a major force in screen-based design from broadcast and interactive online projects to exhibition spaces. Founded in 2000 by creative director Jonathan Notaro, it is a firm that is known for taking creative risks. BNS has supplied branding consultation and design to a range of major multinational corporations, as well as designing the identities and promos for a number of television networks. The firm also partners with advertising agencies and client directly to design and direct commercial spots for broadcast online and on television. BNS has won awards, accolades, and recognition all over the world.

Emirates Airlines

Directed by Jens Gehlhaar, this five-spot brand campaign for one of the world's premier airlines is based on beautifully meandering scripts written by Jennie Morris of Dubai-based Impact BBDO. The spots take the viewer to exotic locations featuring Emirati, Lebanese, Indian, British, French, German, Dutch, Iranian, Syrian, Malaysian, and American actors filmed in trains, planes, automobiles, a cruise ship, and underwater, as well as panoramic aerials. Brand New

School provided a dozen animation and VFX sequences to the spots as well as all Flame finishing and CG sequences.

OfficeMax

The OfficeMax "Life Is Beautiful" commercial spot, created for the advertising agency the Escape Pod, features a world filled with enchantment. Only one woman and a rubber band ball can bring life to an office devoid of color. It is a magical mix of live action and animation that tells a story about living a life that's beautiful. "We seem to like to tell playful stories, straying away from the pretensions often associated with 'serious design,'" says Notaro "The playfulness in our work comes from being in Los Angeles and close to the entertainment industry," notes Gehlhaar. "Content is king, and design doesn't matter in this town. Stories do."

"The greatest creative relationships between Brand New School and clients tend to be based on trust. Once that is established, everyone wins. The irony and frustration peaks when we are called upon as professionals and treated like amateurs. This is where things tend to go sour. For those instances where there is a lack of trust, we have great armor called producers. They provide sound, creative diplomacy by deflecting the bullshit grenades, and telling us when to retreat."

— Jonathan Notaro, creative director/owner, Brand New School

Sharwood's

Directed by Brand New School for McCann Erickson in London, "Go East" is a kaleidoscopic feast for the senses that explodes with action, color, music, and cultural texture. Showcasing Sharwood's line of curry products, it's a whirlwind musical tour of several Eastern regions, including China, India, and Thailand. The piece risks a cross-cultural mash-up of iconography in service of drawing the viewer into an exciting, spicy world. Sean Adams, creative director of AdamsMorioka says of Brand New School's work, "The common thread amidst a list of blue-chip projects is a lightness and a playful attitude that looks deceivingly effortless. It is seductive and unexpected."

Zappos

Nevada-based Zappos is famed as an online shoe retailer that has a "work hard, play hard" mentality and is a success story because of its focus on customer service. However, Zappos sells more than just shoes. Brand New School collaborated with the Ad Store to create a campaign that brought awareness to that fact that Zappos sells accessories and clothes, not just shoes. The enticing "Step Into Zappos" spots have a series of men and women who each enjoy the benefit of a magical Zappos box that dresses them head to toe, with happy results. These transformations are set to upbeat music, incorporating fun, live-action performances and whimsical graphics that send an advertising message while conveying the corporate culture of Zappos.

Soy Joy

The "Battle of the Beans" spot observes an epic battle in the daily workplace. At 3:00 p.m. in offices all around the world, battalions of healthy foods, represented by Soy Joy soybeans, battle it out with armies of sugary snacks. Brand New School (BNS) partnered with the ad agency RPA to develop this commercial spot. Candy fight choreography is the highlight of spots that risks using a counterintuitive dynamic seen in countless superhero movies—the bad guys, jelly beans, are much more fun than the heroes, the soy beans. They're more colorful in the first place, and they start the fight as crazy and amped-up as a bunch of Scottish warriors straight out of the movie *Braveheart* (which was the agency's primary reference for the BNS creative). Only when the sugar crush wanes do the Samurai Soys win the day, and with Zen-like calm, Soy Joy bests the jelly beans.

"Most of the time, we were only asked to 'make something cool,' and that's the best brief ever. It also led to some of our best work."
—Jens Gehlhaar, creative director, Brand New School

Levonelle

For the first-ever UK television spot for the morning-after pill, Brand New School (BNS) created sperms gone wild, a screaming baby, and a sexy chemist, all of which help paint a day in the life of an anxious heroine as she contemplates an accidental condom split. BNS knew they'd have fun with the project when the Levonelle One Step emergency contraception pill's script starred animated sperm. What they didn't expect were the thousands of furious parents calling into radio shows across the UK complaining about the spot. Working with ad agency, MILK, Inc. and Passion Pictures, BNS managed to created a risky concept that was accused of being a "shock advert" that promotes illicit sex. The creative team used a soft pastel palette and a hand-drawn animation style to soften the controversial subject matter. "So far," says Notaro, "no typographers have called into any radio shows criticizing our use of sperm as quotation marks."

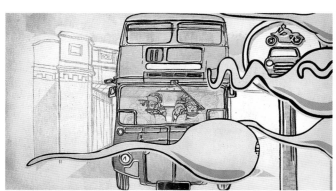

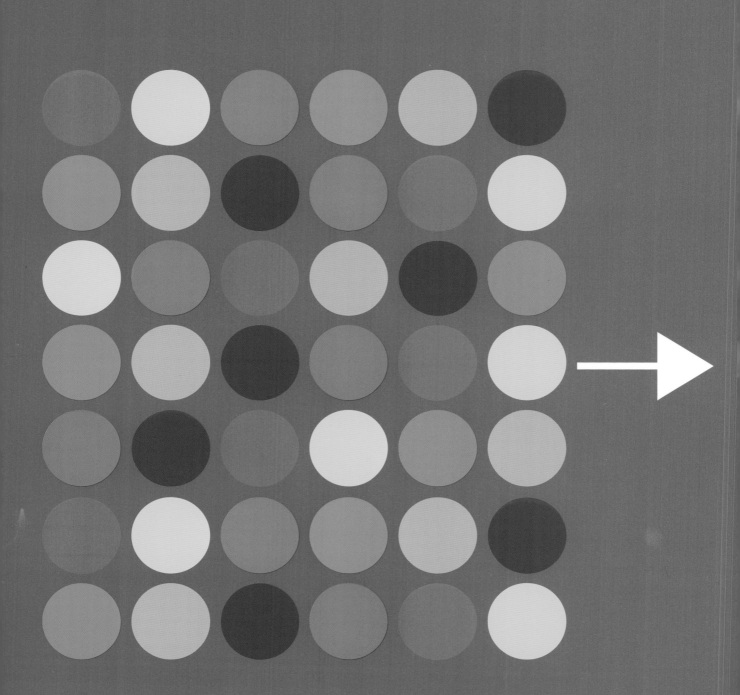

Chapter 6
Creative Briefs

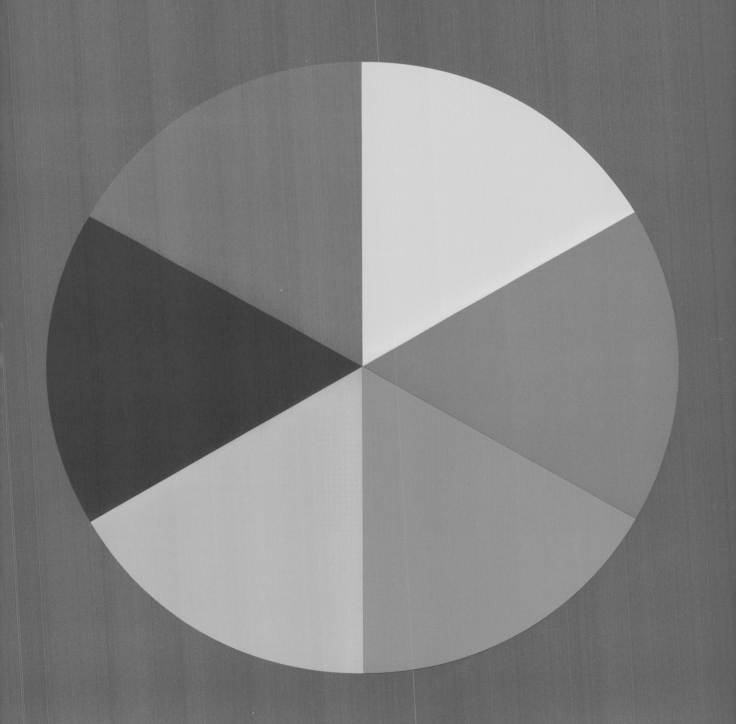

Creative Briefs Are Strategic Tools

Computer scientists have a saying, "Garbage in, garbage out." It means that computers can process a lot of data output, but it will only be as good as the information that was put into the system. It's pretty much the same in design. When creative is developed from great client input, the results can be great. If not, well, it's a recipe for falling short of the mark. Without a well-identified and articulated set of objectives and goals that is rooted in thorough background and research information, a design can't grow out of a solid foundation. There needs to be a summary of all the factors that can impact a design project. It is well worth the time it takes to develop it.

What's in a Creative Brief?

In the best cases, a creative brief is created through meetings, interviews, readings, and discussions between a client and designer. It should contain background information, target audience details, information on competitors, short- and long-term goals, and specific project details. A creative brief will answer these questions:

- What is this project?
- Who is it for?
- Why are we doing it?
- What needs to be done? By whom? By when?
- Where and how will it be used?

Without making a framework for the project, the designer won't be able to understand the parameters or context that needs to be worked within. The creative brief provides an objective strategic tool that can be agreed and acted upon. It can serve as a set of metrics by which to judge and evaluate the appropriateness of a design. At the very least, all the relevant project information is contained within a single document that can be shared as guidelines for the entire client and designer project team.

Negative Impact of No Creative Brief

Any designer who simply launches into a design assignment without a proper briefing doesn't have all the relevant facts and opinions to do a well-informed job. They are also asking for trouble as work progresses. Approvals come with buy in; buy in is so often a result of feeling included and asked for input. Sure, the odds are that they can design something interesting and eye-appealing based on their gut instincts, but these solutions are not grounded in solid understanding, and they are more easily dismissed by both clients and target audiences.

How to Do a Creative Brief

- Develop a list of questions for a client that will provide you with the information you need to proceed with the design.

- Ask the client to identify a list of people in their organization who should participate in the briefing process.

- Do client interview session(s). Meet the selected people one on one for more candid responses. Send clients the questions in advance so that they are better prepared to respond.

- Take notes and/or record the interviews. Having two design team members on hand works better than doing it alone, because it allows the conversation to keep flowing, while still being recorded. Do remember that recording someone without their permission is inappropriate and illegal.

- Compile and analyze the interview findings. Create a summary document. Where is there consensus? Where are the overlaps and tangents?

- Write the creative brief. Include the essential items listed on pages 142–143, and format the document to be easy for both you and the client to use.

- Send the creative brief to the client for approval. Some designers do a design criteria document (see page 146) instead of sending the actual creative brief, which they share only with the design team. Whichever the document, send a summary of findings to the client first before any design begins.

- With client approval, distribute the creative brief to the design team. Some firms do this in a kick-off meeting; others just provide a document. Either way, this is the design team briefing. The creative brief works as the guiding framework and background document to inform all design development.

- Both the client and the design team members should evaluate all design solutions based upon the creative brief. Learn more about evaluating design on pages 164–165.

Project Profile in Creative Briefs
Elizabeth Arden Red Door Spas designed by Alexander Isley, Inc. / Redding, Connecticut

Match: Elizabeth Arden Red Door Spas

Known as an idea-driven design consultancy with a reputation for innovative, influential and effective work, Alexander Isley, Inc., was asked by Elizabeth Arden Salons, Inc. to launch a new brand of hair care products aimed at women thirty to forty-five years old. The assignment included naming the product line, developing the distinct packaging, and designing the in-salon visual merchandising materials. A creative brief was supplied by the client, but was then expanded upon by the designers. Work on the assignment began with a research and positioning phase where positioning, strategy, and brand premise were defined. From this base, a naming commenced with the designers offering a list of brand names and tag lines that corresponded with the agreed upon positioning. The name Match was selected because it emphasized the fact that various products could be combined by customers to create the perfect match for their own hair type. Contained within the client's original brief to the designers was vital information about Elizabeth Arden's U.S. expansion of its upscale Red Door Spas. They had recently acquired the prestigious Mario Tricosi Salons and wished to rebrand these spas and products, including a progressive menu of skin and hair care products, as well a menu of personal care services in a state-of-the-art environment.

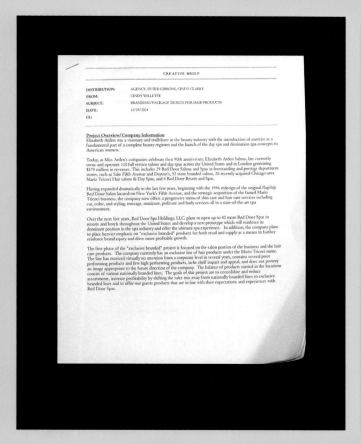

OPPOSITE LEFT
"Our kick-off questionnaire to the client was shorter than usual because they had prepared their own brief," explains creative director Alexander Isley. "Our clients don't usually do this. Nevertheless, we had additional questions and observations." Through interviews with their client, the designers dug deep into the assignment, acquiring information that informed their work.

OPPOSITE RIGHT
The naming criteria developed by Alexander Isley, Inc., is a series of questions that allows the designers and clients to provide background information for exploring a number of potential brand names.

BELOW LEFT
It was in developing the positioning document that the designers decided the product line needed a better name than Portrait, which had been the client's suggestion. "The name conjured up images for us of dusting off an old gilt frame," says Aline Hilford, VP managing director at Alexander Isley, Inc. "We felt there was a better way to approach this audience, starting with a different name—something more modern, light, and engaging."

BELOW RIGHT
Developmental sketches and prototypes that are the beginnings of design development for Match.

Alexander Isley Inc.
9 Brookside Place
Redding, CT 06896
t: (203)544-9692 x-15
f: (203)544-7189
e: aline@alexanderisley.com

A

Brand Name Evaluation

In today's crowded consumer environment, a name has to work hard, and shout loud.
A name is the most visible, influential, repeated and memorable message associated with a brand.
It has emotive and connotative meanings that instantly telegraph brand proposition.
It defines a brand's DNA and growth potential.
It reflects on the parent corporation, and can elevate and enhance the entire brand portfolio.

Checklist:

1. Does the name support corporate objectives?

2. Does the name reinforce existing brand equity?

3. Does the name project the desired brand personality?

4. It is non-category exclusive, leaving room for line extensions or sibling brands?

5. Is the name aspirational? Is it resonant? Does it strike an emotional chord? Is it memorable, fresh, exciting? Does it inspire action, loyalty, interest?

6. Does the name take advantage of current sociological trends/media context? Does the name answer prevalent lifestyle, needs, wants or concerns? Does the name offer a compelling promise or premise to consumers?

7. Does it provide a metaphor for product performance?

8. Does the name appeal to existing customers, and reach out to targeted new consumers?

9. Does the name have media cache and generate PR buzz?

10. Does the name provide a platform for visual/graphic interpretation?

11. Does the name "show well" graphically in current and future destination environments?

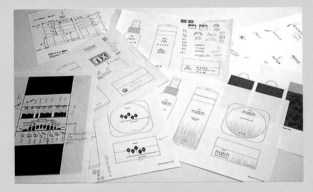

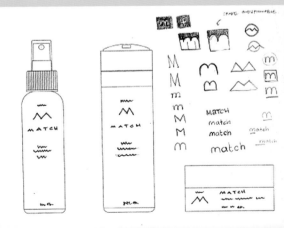

Match: Elizabeth Arden Red Door Spas

The designers created a grid system to compare their client's product with competing brands. Each of the four quadrants represents an attribute, in this case expensive ($$$$) versus cheap ($), and traditional versus trendy, with each brand mapped according to its ranking within these contexts. This kind of four-square grid can compare any two sets of qualifiers a designer wishes. It's an instant way to visually express any client's competitive landscape.

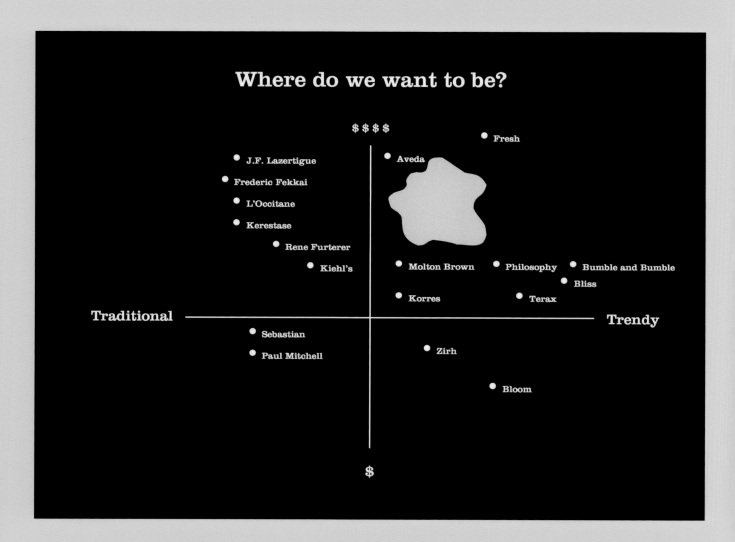

The boards below were used in the strategic development of the Elizabeth Arden Red Door Spas brand. The board (upper left) charts the client's goal in terms of brand positioning by asking the question, "Where do we want to be?" The brand is then plotted according to price point between high-end spas and mid-priced department store brands. The other three boards seen below are mood boards for the Elizabeth Arden Red Door Spas brand—all of which answer the question, "Where do we want to be?" by looking at other factors and influences beyond price. The board at the upper right placed the client's brand in the context of travel, food, and beverage brands; the lower left board places it within consumer products and family brands, while the board at lower right contextualizes Elizabeth Arden Red Door Spas brand with fashion, jewelry, and sports. All three boards identify at a glance the target audience for the new spa brand.

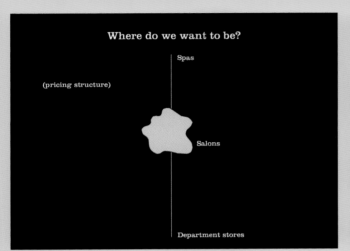

Elizabeth Arden Red Door Spas designed by Alexander Isley, Inc. / Redding, Connecticut

BELOW AND OPPOSITE
A series of design explorations for
Elizabeth Arden's Match. A variety
of color palettes, patterns, packaging shapes, and shelving schemat-
ics are considered.

The process of creating the finished designs for Match included preparing a market gap analysis, competitive audit, and positioning plan. The designers compiled a strategic brief, brand personality document, and launch plan. They then named the line and individual products; designed all packaging; wrote the descriptive copy; and created promotional items, point-of-sale materials, posters, and support literature.

**Some Things We Believe
by Alexander Isley, Inc.**

- We believe you should decide what a design should do before you start to think about what it should look like.
- We believe that there's no such thing as a six-run home run. In today's world, we need to concentrate on hitting singles, keeping our focus on ensuring good short-term results with the knowledge that good long-term benefits will result. We need to focus on being efficient and collaborating with trusted associates. It's the "small ball" approach. OK, enough with the baseball metaphors.
- We believe that with mutual trust, respect, and optimism you get the best work.
- We believe your identity is more than a logo, a typeface, and a color palette.
- We believe that organizations have personalities in the same way that people do, and they are judged in much the same way: By what they say, how they look, and how they behave. We can help with the first two.
- We believe in being honest and efficient and in having a good spirit come through loud and clear.

The 10 Most Important Things to Include in a Creative Brief

1

2

3

4

5

Background Summary.
Who is the client? What is the product or service? What are the strengths, weaknesses, opportunities, and threats, or SWOT. Research, reports, and any other documents that help you understand the situation.

Overview.
What is the project? What are we designing and why? Why do we need this project? What's the opportunity?

Drivers.
What is our goal for this project? What are we trying to achieve? What is the purpose of our work? What are our top three objectives?

Audience.
Who are we talking to? What do they think of us? Why should they care?

Competitors.
Who is the competition? What are they telling the audience that we should be telling them? SWOT analysis on them? What differentiates us from them?

6 7 8 9 10

Tone.
How should we be communicating? What adjectives describe the feeling or approach?

Message.
What are we saying with this piece exactly? Are the words already developed or do we need to develop them? What do we want audiences to take away?

Visuals.
Are we developing new images or picking up existing ones? If we are creating them, who, what, where are we shooting? And why?

Details.
Any mandatory info? List of deliverables? Preconceived ideas? Format parameters? Limitations and restrictions? Timeline, schedule, budget?

People.
Who are we reporting to? Who exactly is approving this work? Who needs to be informed of our progress? By what means?

Project Profile in Creative Briefs

Logan Collection Vail designed by Aufuldish & Warinner, graphic designers / San Anselmo, California

Impulse: **Logan Collection Vail Interview with Bob Aufuldish, creative director / partner**

Q. Please describe the client, along with their product/service:
A. The project is for the Logan Collection Vail, collectors of contemporary art.

Q. What was your brief on this project? What were you asked to do?
A. Design a book of the Logans' extensive collection of works on paper.

Q. Who is the audience for this project?
A. Broadly speaking, it's the art world.

Q. What exactly is this piece? What is its purpose? How is it used by the client?
A. The Logans use the books to document their collection and to build awareness about it. They want to raise the profile of this aspect of their collection. As Kent Logan states in

his opening essay, "Their importance to us is related to the fact that drawings often capture that first extemporaneous thought of the artist."

Q Why does it look the way it does?
A. A number of reasons. I previously designed a book, *Postmodern Portraiture*, from their collection. One of the requests was that this new volume relate to the previous one.

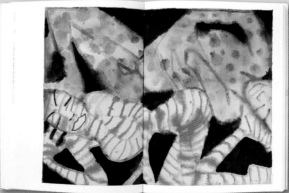

The size is the same, and so are a few of the typefaces used, but the grid and the way the material is organized is different. *Impulse* is organized around thematic groupings, with each differentiated by a section opening spread. There are enough ribbons bound into the book so that each section and the opening essay can be individually bookmarked. In a book of this length [270 pages], I find that it's especially important to pay attention to navigation issues. The design shows the works as large as possible, and the uneven edges of the paper are shown when appropriate. We took the extra effort to carefully silhouette the works where the irregular edges of the paper are an important part of the work.

OPPOSITE
The cover and a spread from *Postmodern Portraiture*.

BELOW
The cover and two spreads from *Impulse*.

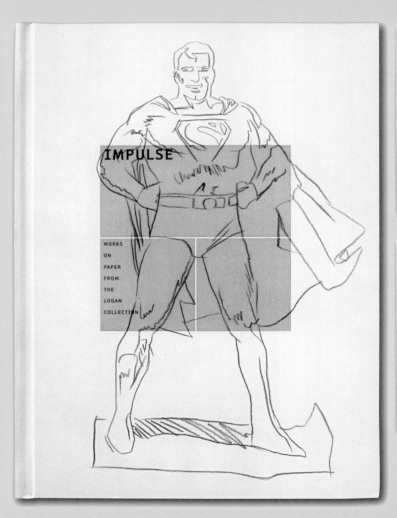

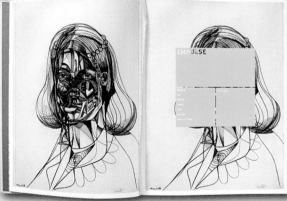

Managing to a Creative Brief

A creative brief is used not only at the start of a project, but throughout the entire design process. It is the one constant element that has been agreed upon and is objective enough to act as a guideline. Clients primarily use it to get organized, and to develop consensus within their own enterprises. They then use it to determine if the design actually solves the problem it was intended to. Designers use creative briefs to fact-find and understand their client, building knowledge about both perception and reality of the problem at hand. Designers often find out that what their client thinks is the problem is not the problem at all. These are the things that become revealed in the briefing.

Once the creative brief is agreed upon by both the designer and client, it is a useful tool for getting all members of the design team on board and ready to work on the project. The designers have relevant grounding to inform their thinking, the copywriter has messaging information, the production and project managers have milestones and due dates, and the account executive has met and bonded with all client stakeholders. Everyone has what they need to work, no matter what their responsibility is.

Creative Briefs vs. Design Criteria

Sometimes, designers take the extra step of translating a creative brief provided by their clients into a design criteria. If a creative brief is a tool that provides a framework and roadmap for a design project, the design criteria is the summary of the approach and a preplan for the creative. The design criteria describes what the designer will do to solve the problem—i.e., the creative strategy.

Taking the time to develop design criteria is very important if the client is contradictory or indecisive. It gives the designers another opportunity to clarify details before they begin creative work by team members who tend to be the most highly skilled and most expensive in terms of hourly rate. It creates a sureness that designer and client are in agreement.

What's Included in a Design Criteria

Overview:
• Who they are [the client? the audience?]
• What the problem is (they say)
• What the problem is (really)

Research/Analysis Summary:
• What are they doing?
• What are others doing?

Approach:
• What we are recommending be done
• Design overview (brief statement about what needs to be done)

Client Sign Off:
• Approval to proceed with design. This is a critical step, if ever needed later as evidence of client approval in the case of things turning sour in a project.

Who Uses a Creative Brief?

Both the client and the design team use the creative brief. Creating it helps a client crystallize the salient information, gather their thoughts, and research and identify goals and objectives. It provides an opportunity for all stakeholders to give input and have their say. It aids in client buy in of the resulting designs mostly because the client team has all provided input.

For the designer, the brief provides relevant information to alleviate guesswork. Who knows the client's business better than the client? By gathering this information concisely in one document, the creative brief is a criteria for evaluation, outlining metrics that indicate success, and ultimately holding the designer accountable—unless of course, the designer can convince their client that the creative brief is wrong.

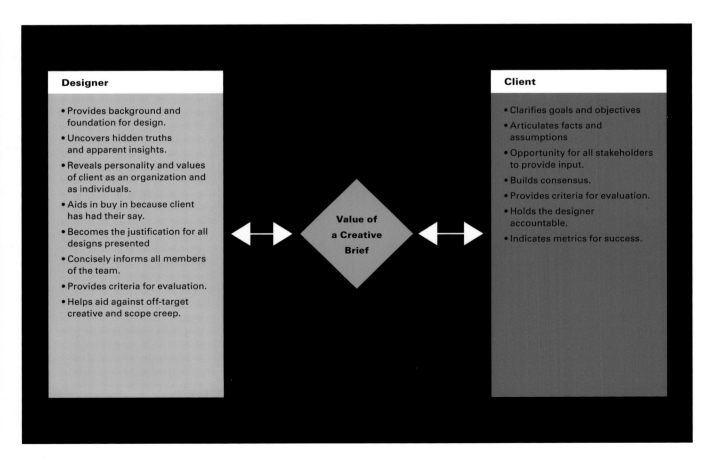

Designer

- Provides background and foundation for design.
- Uncovers hidden truths and apparent insights.
- Reveals personality and values of client as an organization and as individuals.
- Aids in buy in because client has had their say.
- Becomes the justification for all designs presented
- Concisely informs all members of the team.
- Provides criteria for evaluation.
- Helps aid against off-target creative and scope creep.

Value of a Creative Brief

Client

- Clarifies goals and objectives
- Articulates facts and assumptions
- Opportunity for all stakeholders to provide input.
- Builds consensus.
- Provides criteria for evaluation.
- Holds the designer accountable.
- Indicates metrics for success.

Going without a Creative Brief

Project Profile in Creative Briefs
SPIN! Neapolitan Pizza designed by
Willoughby Design / Kansas City, Missouri

There are times when a formal creative briefing session, followed by a typewritten and comprehensive creative brief may not be necessary. The two main reasons are

- The assignment is a continuation of a larger program that the designer has already been working on. It may have had a formal creative brief at the start of the working relationship and now, with a wealth of experience having worked on a previous design, a new creative brief may not be needed. In essence, it is a project that falls within a larger, earlier creative brief.

- The client trusts the designer implicitly. They have worked together over the course of many years or many projects and, thus, have developed a kind of telepathy from such a close working relationship. The designer intuitively understands the client, their product or service, their competition, and their customer extremely well. This allows the client to state their problem or goal and then give the designer carte blanche to design as they see fit.

Both of these conditions involve trust and an extensive working relationship. Beginning design without being properly briefed under other circumstances is usually a recipe for disaster. The designer has no objective criteria on which to have their work evaluated. Mostly, they have not received adequate information as preparation for their work in the first place.

SPIN! Neapolitan Pizza

Willoughby Design is a brand design and innovation firm made up of strategists, designers, and writers. They work in flexible teams, assigning the appropriate mix of talent to each project. All of their team members believe that every unique brand experience starts with a story. The firm specializes in bringing companies and products to consumers through emotionally centered visual storytelling that leaves lasting impressions and creates brand believers. This philosophy and approach is evident in their work for Spin! Pizza.

Willoughby loves designing retail experiences that bring every element together to create a memorable encounter for customers. Gail Lozoff, owner of Einstein Bros. Bagels, as well as Bagel and Bagel, has been a partner with Willoughby for over fifteen years, in leading fast-casual restaurant innovations. Lozoff's newest concept, Spin!—inspired by Neapolitan-style pizza and her love for Italian cycling—is a *favoloso* fast-casual restaurant experience that is poised for national expansion. Because of the longstanding working relationship between designer and client, no formal creative brief was prepared.

The work on Spin! included a vision workshop, positioning, brand identity and standards, collateral, environmental graphics, signage, and interactive components. After a successful two-year engagement designing the identity and store concept for the first location, Willoughby is working with Spin! to open five new stores in the Kansas City area with plans for a national launch close behind.

THIS PAGE
Willoughby Design worked in collaboration with client Gail Lozoff,
Hammerpress letterpress studio,
and 360° Architects to craft the first
favoloso pizza concept restaurant
of its kind.

Spin! Neapolitan Pizza designed by Willoughby Design / Kansas City, Missouri

Spin! Neapolitan Pizza

Rich tapestries of letterpress graphics, authentic Italian pizza, and bicycling converge for this new fast-casual restaurant concept. This dadaist coupling of bicycles and pizza play out in the name and is a marriage of the owner's two loves. Bicycle-inspired details include using gears on light fixtures and a bike rail for the outdoor patio railing.

A letterpress artist created the artwork that was composed into two murals that bookend the space. Three posts rise from the center to hold the menu boards. Each graphic item from the identity to the signage imparts hand-done, rich layering, just like the pizza.

Chapter 7
Aesthetic Considerations

Aesthetics in Design

When many people think of design, what they are actually conjuring up in their minds is something much more analogous to "style"—the look of the thing, not its rationale or technical configuration. Clients react to the design in either a positive or negative way. Designers need to explain design in terms of how a particular arrangement of graphic elements works together to communicate something to an audience that will help the client solve their problem or reach their goal. They need to present the work in terms of aesthetics, not just mere appearance. These two terms are not exactly synonymous.

What Is Aesthetics?

Aesthetics comes from the Greek word for *perceiver* or *sensitive*. Aesthetics is the theory and study of beauty. As the old saying goes, "beauty is in the eye of the beholder." Everything we experience in life shapes our idea of beauty—essentially, what is pleasing is a learned response. Each and every one of us goes through cultural training—intentional or unintentional—that forms our ideas of what is aesthetically pleasing. In philosophical terms, aesthetics is also the study of sensory or "sensori-emotional" value, a meaning that refers to the sensibilities of perception, or the idea of intuition. Essentially, how something is viewed and perceived by a person causes them to place a particular value judgment upon it.

Design Aesthetics

Aesthetics in design has to do with the deliberate arrangement of elements—shape, color, typography, etc.—in a way that appeals to the senses and/or emotions. It is an expression of taste, which is essentially a preference. Taste is personal, but also subject to social pressures. A particular group declares something to be in "good" or "bad" taste, and if a person is part of that group, they tend to agree with the group opinion. Why this all matters is that at the heart of a designer's work is encoding and decoding messages to move a particular group of people or target audience to do something. This encoding and decoding means translating ideas from client speak into audience speak, or translating client goals into visual imagery—essentially, translating information from one format into the other. Therefore, designers must understand the tastes of the target audience and then leverage aesthetics to mirror those preferences. So to come full circle, when people say that design is all about surface appearance, they are missing the deeper understanding that those surfaces are created to form aesthetic or emotional and sensory connections.

Not Personal Preferences

When designers solve visual problems, they must reach past their own personal aesthetic preferences to tap into those of their audience. One of the biggest challenges a designer faces is helping their client do the same thing. This is why all design decisions must be argued as appropriate for a specific context, not just that it looks and feels good or "works." That may be true, but this opens the door to endless subjective critique by the client. Traditionally that is something that does not result in approval, intact, of a designer's original well-considered concept.

In this way, the effective use of aesthetic choices can make a design resonate deeply with a target audience. This resonance creates an emotional connection. For example, the cover of a baking book incorporates rich autumn colors and a large central image of a pie. The target audience is drawn to the book, recalling festive and warm family gatherings, and buys the book. It's a simple example, but, a compelling and useful one. When the same autumn palette is then applied to the packaging for other ancillary products, the connection is made over and over again.

Aesthetic Universals

The New Zealand–based philosopher Denis Dutton, author of the 2009 book, *The Art Instinct: Beauty, Pleasure, and Human Evolution*, has identified seven universal signatures in human aesthetics. These things are common, no matter what cultural difference may be. In summary, Dutton observes the following identifying characteristics:

1

Expertise or virtuosity.
Technical artistic skills are cultivated, recognized, and admired.

2

Nonutilitarian pleasure.
People enjoy art for art's sake and don't demand that it be functional.

3

Style.
Artistic objects satisfy rules of composition that position them within a recognizable category or style.

4

Criticism.
Works of art are judged, appreciated, or interpreted

5

Imitation.
Works of art simulate experiences of the world.

6

Special focus.
Art is apart from ordinary life.

7

Imagination.
Artists and their audiences conjure hypothetical worlds in their minds.

Project Profile in Aesthetic Considerations: AdamsMorioka, Inc.

Annenberg Community Beach House designed by AdamsMorioka, Inc. / Beverly Hills, CA • New York, New York USA

AdamsMorioka is a graphic design firm with offices in Beverly Hills, California, and New York City, founded by Sean Adams and Noreen Morioka in 1994. Their work ranges from corporate identities, identity systems, print campaigns, and environmental graphics, to motion and digital projects, animation, and websites. The firm's founding philosophy of clarity, purity, and resonance spearheaded a revolution in the design community from chaos and complexity to honesty and simplicity and continues to drive their work today.

The Annenberg Community Beach House

The Annenberg Community Beach House at Santa Monica State Beach is a public facility with clublike amenities located on five acres of oceanfront property. It sits on a site which was once the opulent private estate that newspaper magnate William Randolph Hearst purchased for his movie star paramour Marion Davies. Later,

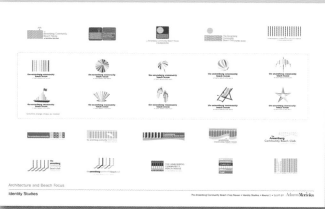

the property became the Sand & Sea Club, a limited-membership beach club. Although only the guest cottage and pool remain from the original structures, an extensive ten-year restoration resulted in new beach recreation areas, tennis and volleyball courts, a snack bar, and meeting and event rooms. AdamsMorioka created the identity, the wayfinding, ADA, and informational signage system for the Beach House.

OPPOSITE AND BELOW
AdamsMorioka developed a unifying theme of lively stripes of color for the Annenberg Community Beach House's extensive slate of public spaces. A crisp palette and simple sand and surf iconography informs guests and identifies the property. The identity was presented to the client, as well as to the public attending governmental review meetings, in a series of boards that walk through the look and feel of the branding.

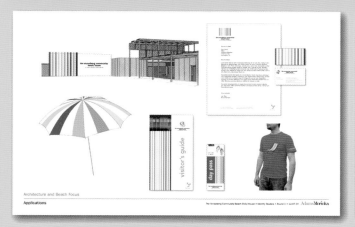

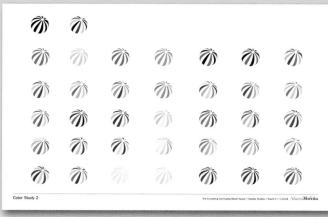

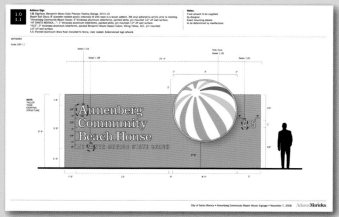

Annenberg Community Beach House designed by AdamsMorioka, Inc. / Beverly Hills, CA • New York, New York USA

BELOW AND OPPOSITE
AdamsMorioka worked with the city of Santa Monica, the Annenberg Foundation (which provided an endowment for the facility), and Frederick Fisher Partners, architects on the project. Taking cues from both the original Hearst architect, Julia Morgan, and Fisher's work, AdamsMorioka developed a vibrant color palette and kinetic system of interchangeable beach-inspired icons that anchor the identity. The design revolves around the idea of stripes, which echo the verticality of the new freestanding pool house column structures, as well as the many palm trees that surround the property.

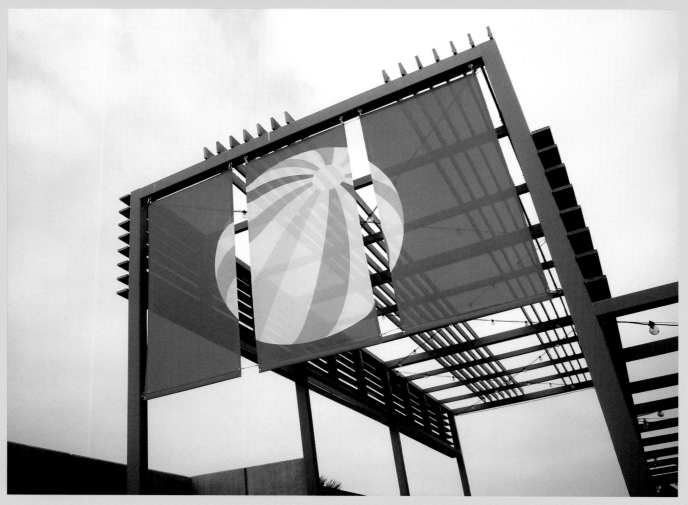

"The color palette is based on the rare handmade Malibu tiles selected by Julia Morgan for the original estate," explains Sean Adams. "These tiles were some of the few remaining elements from Marion Davies and we wanted to incorporate her spirit in the new incarnation of the Beach House." A clear cerulean blue dominates the palette, references the open sky and ocean, and contrasts nicely with the other colors in the palette that respects the heritage of the facility.

"The identity and signage follow a beach club attitude," says Adams. "It is a public facility. However, we wanted the Annenberg Community Beach House to have the feeling of an exclusive club, yet accessible." All of the signage is based on either the Golden Rectangle or a circle. The ADA (Americans With Disabilities Act) safety signage, above, looks like a series of beach towels hung on a fence to dry. All of the typography needed to be very large in scale to meet ADA requirements, so the designers had to work to create pleasing proportions in the signage.

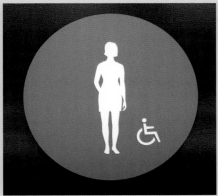

POOL RULES

For the safety and enjoyment of all pool guests:

- Swimmers must shower before entering the water
- Swim suits or equivalent must be worn in the water
- Children under age 12 must be accompanied and supervised by an adult at all times
- Children under age 8 and under 4' in height must be accompanied by an adult in the water at all times
- Children requiring diapers must wear a swim diaper in the water

POOL RULES

The following are prohibited:

- Running, rough play, pushing or dunking of others
- Bikes, scooters, skates, skateboards
- Glass containers
- Masks, fins or snorkels during recreational swim
- Toys in the water, unless distributed by Beach House staff
- Flotation devices (except Coast Guard approved lifejackets)

Guests must abide by the decision of Beach House staff regarding the interpretation of any rules governing the use of this facility. Any behavior or activity determined by the staff to be unsafe, hazardous, inappropriate or a violation of the rules is prohibited.

MAXIMUM OCCUPANCY 113

WARNING: NO LIFEGUARD ON DUTY

Children under the age of 14 should not use pool without an adult in attendance.

NO DIVING ALLOWED

IN CASE OF EMERGENCY CALL 911

ARTIFICIAL RESPIRATION

1. Call 911 — 911
2. Tilt head, lift chin, check breathing
3. Give two breaths
4. Position hands on the center of chest
5. Firmly push down 2 inches on the chest 30 times
6. Continue with 2 breaths and 30 pumps until help arrives

Well-Designed Goes Beyond Pretty

Great design can be pretty. If pretty is the right way to deliver the right message to the right people, then by all means, a designer should make their work pretty. It's all about connecting an audience to a client's product or service. Design at its best uses all the artistic and aesthetic tools possible to do the job it was intended to do.

Aesthetic Truths

Aesthetics plays a significant role in cognitive processing—the way things look and feel affects the way people think or understand them. Consider the following truths when thinking about how a design can move an audience to a particular response:

- **Aesthetics can communicate function and the idea of usability.**
- **People believe they like what they like instinctively—but, in fact, it is a learned preference.**
- **Color affects people on a visceral level.**
- **Emotions are strong differentiators because they trigger unconscious responses to the design for a product or service.**
- **People identify and trust certain personalities. Because personality can be conveyed through branding, people perceive a client's personality through graphics.**

In 2002, Donald A. Norman, professor of cognitive and computer science, author of the books *The Design of Everyday Things* (2002) and *Emotional Design: Why We Love (Or Hate) Everyday Things* (2005), wrote in an article for *Interactions* magazine, "Aesthetics matter: attractive things work better." He goes on to essentially argue that beauty, as well as function and usability, are of equal and necessary importance in design. Norman's work is valuable to designers because he breaks down the psychology behind what people think of as "good" and "bad" design—all helpful ammunition in conversations justifying a particular design solution to a client.

So, if we understand that emotion (feeling) and cognition (thinking) are both at work in design to create perception (intuitive knowing), then having all three things addressed by the designer, in the context of their target audience, is how to move design beyond the merely visual into a deeper meaning. When that happens, a design concept will strike a true and lasting chord with the audience.

Aesthetic Components

Some of the most important aesthetic
components in graphic design include
the following:

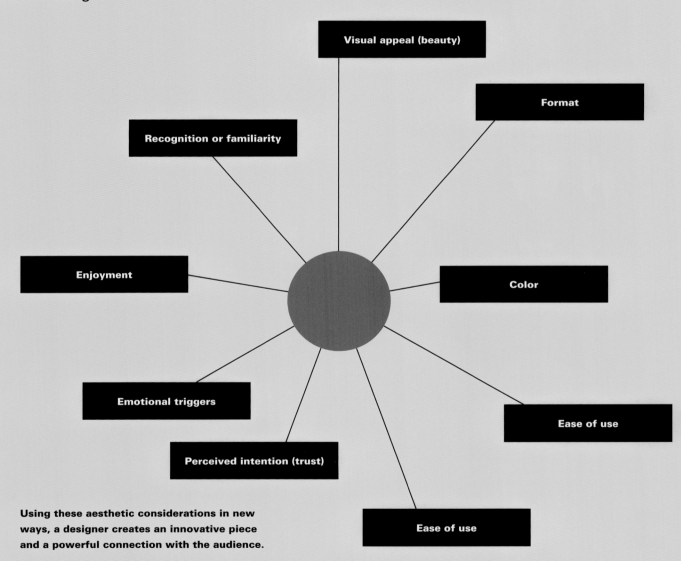

Visual appeal (beauty)

Format

Recognition or familiarity

Enjoyment

Color

Emotional triggers

Ease of use

Perceived intention (trust)

Ease of use

**Using these aesthetic considerations in new
ways, a designer creates an innovative piece
and a powerful connection with the audience.**

Mapping Aesthetics

It can be useful to visualize the aesthetic considerations of design solutions. Why? It gives a designer and a client a quick visual reference about the emphasis being placed on particular aesthetic factors. It lets the designer know if their solutions are different enough to provide a range of choices for the client. (Of course, a range may or may not be desirable for some projects.)

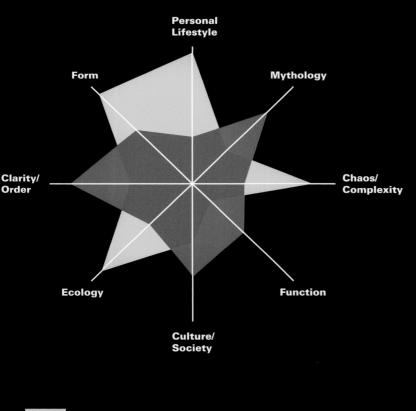

 Design Solution 1

 Design Solution 2

Understanding Aesthetic Dynamics in Design

Psychologists, philosophers, and designers all study aesthetics. There are numerous theories and schools of thought on the specific details on how to use aesthetics and how it fits into the way people think and feel, or to use a fancy way of saying it, the cognitive-effective framework.

There is a duality in responding to the differences between thinking and feeling, yet both must be addressed by the designer. For example, how much order provides coherence before it becomes boring to a certain group of people? How much complexity provides an intriguing puzzle that requires audience involvement? How long before that involvement frustrates them and the audience moves on to an easier, more apparent format? The line between these polar opposites seems to be always in flux—ask a different group of people, and get a different answer. This is where a designer really earns their fees. First by understanding, then by graphically interpreting the aesthetic requirements of the audience they are designing for, is one of the key strengths a designer must have. This is what separates a technician from an artist or a good designer from a great one.

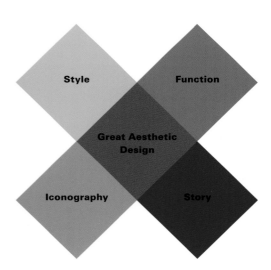

ABOVE
Great aesthetic design lives at the intersection of four main factors: style, function, story, and iconography. Balancing these within the specific context the design will be used in allows the target audience to make an intellectual and emotional connection with the client's message.

Key Aesthetic Questions

If a designer boils it all down to the essential, there are a few critical questions they need answered in terms of aesthetic considerations. These questions refer back to the primary questions asked during the designer's creative briefing session. They include

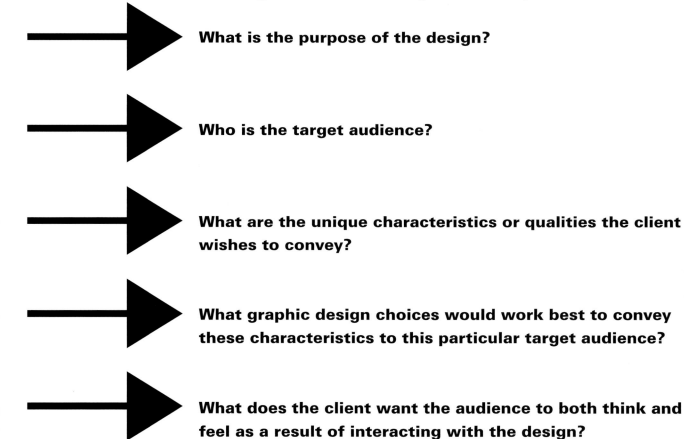

What is the purpose of the design?

Who is the target audience?

What are the unique characteristics or qualities the client wishes to convey?

What graphic design choices would work best to convey these characteristics to this particular target audience?

What does the client want the audience to both think and feel as a result of interacting with the design?

How will we know that the audience is reacting like we want them to?

Case Study in Aesthetic Considerations

Modern Dog Design Company / Seattle, Washington USA

Founded in Seattle Washington in 1987 by Robynne Raye and Michael Strassburger, Modern Dog Design Co. creates intriguing, thought provoking, and often quite cheeky design in interactive and print medias. "Right from the start, if a job came along that we didn't think we would enjoy, we turned it down—even when we really needed money," says Strassburger. "We always said to ourselves, 'What if a really fun job comes in and we're stuck doing this?' That screening process was a key factor in our development as a company." That philosophy has lead to a variety of projects, including branding, identity, product development, illustration, custom lettering, publication design, websites, character design, and naming in an array of stylistic approaches for a broad range of clients.

At the heart of Modern Dog Design Company's work is what Raye describes as "bold, imaginative, and playful design." It is diverse, and nearly always exhibits a razor sharp sense of humor. Famed graphic designer Rick Valicenti wryly observed that their work "is the complete archaeological core sample of late twentieth century or maybe earlier American graphics."

Fainting Goat Gelato

Fainting Goat is a family-owned and run organic gelato shop located in the Wallingford neighborhood of Seattle. Their gelato is made from locally grown, organic dairy and sugar, and is handcrafted on site. Lower in both fat and calories when compared to traditional ice cream, it's a lighter and healthier sweet treat. Modern Dog designed their identity and store signage with aesthetics that reflect the handmade quality of the gelato itself.

K2 Japan

"In the early '90s we were introduced to K2 Japan through our affiliation with K2 Snowboards here in the US," notes Strassburger. "The people at K2 Japan who hired us thought our work looked very West Coast American. For several years, we designed their skis and collateral materials—we even designed and wrote a comic book that was used as a giveaway." The comic book proved to be so successful that the characters Modern Dog designed (left) were turned into life-size costumes and made live appearances at Japanese retailers and trade shows. Aesthetically, these designs proved so popular that they launched scores of imitators, making Modern Dog's designs the dominant visual language for winter snow sport gear in Asia. This cross-cultural exchange was an interesting working experience. "When we initially traveled to Japan to work on a line of skis with them,' says Raye, "we were not prepared for the culture shock. If you've ever seen the movie *Lost in Translation*, then you have a pretty good mental picture of what that was like. But we did have a lot of fun, and we are proud of all this work."

Phinney Neighborhood Associates

This poster is for the Phinney Home Tour, an event produced by the Phinney Neighborhood Association (PNA) in the Seattle area.

Modern Dog has done many posters for the PNA over the years, including ones for their Artwalk and Garden Tours. "Our goal was to capture both themes in the poster," explains Raye. "In the past, the home tour posters have usually featured a photograph of a house on the tour. The bird is looking at the little house and wondering if he can get a look inside it. In case you're wondering, his friend Mr. Hummingbird lives there."

Olive

Olive is dedicated to featuring the largest variety of healthful and environmentally friendly dog products available online and beyond. Modern Dog has worked with Olive founders Gina Quiroga and Barb Savidge for several years launching the brand and creating everything from packaging to email marketing blasts. "I had no experience with

graphic design," says Quiroga. "But from the very beginning Modern Dog included us in the process. As we went along, the dialogue led to a broad range of Olive-branded goods. We agreed to a financial arrangement that allows them to participate in our success and allows us access to their exceptional skills. We couldn't be happier."

Modern Dog named, as well as designed, a variety of products for Austin, Texas–based Olive. "Some of our favorites include Soap Lump, Fur Spritzer, and Bubble + Squeak organic dog shampoo, " says Raye. "It's great to work with a company that truly cares about our environment and not only talks the talk, but walks the walk. Olive

Modern Dog helped create this company's identity from the ground up. They developed a friendly dog character, which is central to the identity system. One of the central messages all of the designs for Olive must express is that they are makers of "Green Goods for Modern Dogs."

spa products contain nothing yucky—no parabens, no sodium lauryl/laureth sulfates, no phthalates—and are completely biodegradable." The muslin bag is imprinted with the lovable Olive logo. The products are guaranteed to be gentle on dogs and the Earth, something the design also conveys aesthetically.

Monthly e-blasts created by Modern Dog have proven to be an effective marketing technique for Olive. "To help save money and time, we designed three templates that can be used repeatedly," explains Strassburger. "Since most of Olive's sales are driven by their online store, the e-blasts are an important part of their business: sales

always spike immediately following their release. We have the process streamlined and now most e-blasts only take a couple of hours to complete." The designers even use their own dogs as models—that's Raye's Cairn Terrier, Conan, left.

GREEN GOODS
FOR MODERN DOGS

October is Adopt-a-Dog Month

Established by the <u>American Humane Association</u>, Adopt-a-Dog Month promotes dog adoptions from animal shelters and educates people about responsible pet care. The hope is that more people will open their homes and hearts to a shelter dog either through permanent adoption, volunteering their time, donating money, or fostering dogs awaiting adoption. If you do decide to adopt, here are a few tips for figuring out your new pet. (Plus some valuable savings.)

Getting to Know You

It's natural to expect some period of mutual adjustment when bringing a dog into your home. To make the transition as smooth as possible consider the following:

1. Build a 'Healthcare team'. Just like you, your dog will have different healthcare needs—emergency, primary and holistic. It's important that you find healthcare professionals you like and that are capable of meeting your expectations—before you actually need them.

2. Feed your new 'dog' a nutritious diet --most new owners appreciate the convenience of natural or <u>organic dry food</u> and later consider a wet, dehydrated or raw frozen diet, all of which are more expensive—and a little less convenient--but healthier than kibble.

3. Use healthful treats for reward-based training. Don't be surprised if at first your new pooch has a 'low' level of interest in food or treats. Stress might be a potential explanation for a dog's failure to take treats or respond to you initially. Give it time, well-timed, <u>healthful treats</u> can reinforce the behaviors you want your dog to repeat.

4. Be patient, it may take awhile for your pet to adjust to its new home and to feel secure in knowing that the world's an overall safe place.

Grizzly Salmon Oil
Rich in Omega-3's and 6's and derived from only wild Alaskan Salmon, Grizzly all-natural Salmon Oil™, helps your dog maintain optimum health and overall vitality.

West Paw Bumper Bed
A perfect place to call their own; filled with thick densely woven 100% recycled IntelliLoft™ polyfill that will not bunch or flatten even with extreme use over time.

Pecks Dog Treats
Bite-size buffalo and blueberry treats, Pecks are perfect for training—quick to serve and easy to munch during practice sessions for obedience, agility and other canine activities.

Give a Dog a Home. And save 10% off your next Olive order.
CODE: ADOPTADOG
Check out the <u>Ecocettera/Sale Section</u>—coupon good on Sale Stuff too!
Offer expires Tuesday, October 7

GREEN GOODS
FOR MODERN DOGS

The **dog days of summer** are filled with travel, leisure and plenty of outdoor activity. Portable bowls, travel food and snacks, poop bags and clean-up wipes are must - haves when on the go.

First Day at the Beach
Ducky, Fire Island

Take Off
For air travel, look for airline-standard or airline-approved carriers that can be worn over the shoulder and that fully enclose your pet with plenty of ventilation (and style).

Pick Up
Be prepared with Olive biode-gradable, GMO-free corn poop bags available in two convenient sizes-- Unisex and Super Poop. Plus the cool art canister means you don't have to keep your bags out of sight.

Rest Up
Give your furry friend a place of their own when away from home. Made from 85% recycled IntelliLoft fibers, Eco Nap is environmentally friendly and provides dogs and cats with familiar territory anywhere they go.

Scrub Up
Transform your backyard to an al fresco Spa with a Tubtrugs Flexible tubs made from 100% post industrial waste, a more environmentally friendly alternative to other wash tubs.

Drink Up
Good hydration is important when traveling. Lightweight and compact collapsible bowls make on-the-road rehydration a breeze.

Wipe Up
Made from the high quality pure lavender essential oils, Herban Essentials Pet Tow-elettes are naturally antibacterial and antiseptic, making wipe-ups on the go and in the car a cinch.

Extend your dollars during the dog days of Summer.
Save 12% off your entire order.
Input code: DOGDAYS at checkout.
Offer ends May 26, 2009 | www.olivegreendog.com

Evaluating Aesthetic Choices

Presenting a design and explaining the aesthetic considerations and creative decisions in a business/audience context is a great way to increase a designer's approval ratings. However, it is not a certainty that the design will be accepted. That still takes great presentation and persuasion skills. Selling a design and getting approvals every time is something a designer gets better and better at the more they do it.

Managing the Conversation

When presenting any design, make sure to discuss the following. These tips keep the conversation at a level that emphasizes the designer as a skilled professional consultant and not an exotic artist:

- How this design positions the client in their competitive landscape
- The client's business goals and how this design helps meet them
- The audience's needs, expectations, aspirations and how this design works to satisfy them
- The overall tone and content and how it supports the client's message(s)
- Feasibility: how this design will be rolled out on time and on budget
- New opportunities that presented themselves in the course of developing this design

Avoid discussions that focus on the following:

- Minutia of graphic choices
- Personal preferences
- Reactions not based on the creative brief

Getting Clients to Participate

A designer should encourage both positive and negative feedback from the client. If the client expresses resistance to a particular design, make sure to explore their concerns with professionalism and an open mind. Remember that the client usually knows their business and their consumers better. Their gut instinct that a design misses the mark must be considered and weighed appropriately.

Sometimes, clients have difficulty speaking the language of design and aesthetics. It is not in the realm of their comfort zone. It can be kind of like speaking a foreign language. Therefore, clients are often unable, or unwilling, to provide clear feedback. It's up to the designer or open them up and encourage them to try to articulate what the pluses and minuses of a particular design are for them.

Avoid the Negatives

One of the biggest mistakes a designer can make is arguing with the client. The designer has been paid to do a job, they do it to the best of their ability, and they present it to their client in the best way they can. If the client doesn't believe it solves their problem or addresses their needs, it is up to the designer to convince them. Sometimes, however, it is simply impossible. No matter how eloquently the designer presents the work or how passionately they argue the design's appropriateness, the client just doesn't agree, or maybe, they simply don't like it.

In order for the designer to not get caught in an endless loop of revisions and/or the creation of new concepts, it is critical to have clear feedback in order to know how to proceed. It is also critical to have indicated in the contract for the project, right up front, how many revisions are included in the designer's fee. Sometimes, if a designer fails to argue their design solution effectively, they can fall back on contractual limitations to get their design approved. In that instance, the client is forced to accept a design, or increase the designer's fee, in order to see additional solutions. That's not a great situation to be in. It is far better to argue the design convincingly and get the client to agree wholeheartedly.

Soliciting Feedback

Some helpful suggestions on getting clients to provide meaningful and useful feedback are:

Don't make assumptions: → Go into the session with an open mind.

Listen, listen, listen: → Let the client say what he wants to say.

Don't interrupt: → Designers often feel defensive and stop the flow of conversation prematurely.

Clarify: → Repeat what the client has said to make sure it's understood.

Ask questions: → Follow up on client comments by asking for additional information.

Go into the details: → Make sure that it is clear exactly what the concern is. Really.

Postpone judgments: → Don't immediately dismiss what seems like a bad comment from the client.

Take it on board: → Tell the client you'll think over the feedback and get back to them.

Thank them: → Make sure to maintain civility and a pleasant working relationship, even if you disagree with their feedback.

Think about who pays the bills: → Ultimately, the client is the boss. They get to have it their way.

Maintain your relationship: → Clients hire designers that they enjoy working with.

Project Profile in Aesthetic Considerations
Ogilvy Albania & Kosova

Newborn designed by Ogilvy Albania & Kosova / Tirana, Republic of Albania, Prishtina, Kosovo

Newborn: Kosovo
Independence Monument

Under the creative direction of Fisnik Ismaili, Ogilvy Albania & Kosova are part of Ogilvy & Mather Worldwide Network of advertising agencies. The firm is devoted to creative production and innovative use of media, and specializes in advertising, branding and identity, graphic design, interactive media, public relations, promotions, and event and media management. All this expertise came into use on the creation of the Newborn Monument. Ten days before the actual event, Ogilvy came up with the idea to prepare a celebration for the biggest day in their country—the Declaration of Independence in 2008. The challenge was to avoid any instance that would uproar the crowd and yet provide a joyful manifestation that would mark this historical day. The result was the creation of a large, 9-ton interactive sculpture that became a symbol and focal point for the day. Over 150,000 people wrote on it, starting with the president and the prime minister.

Ogilvy chose the word "newborn" to encapsulate everything that the independence was going to bring to the country, in one word. They intentionally used an English word to globally communicate a new country being born. "It was an extremely emotional project," says Ismaili. "A once-in-a-lifetime piece of work." The project has won numerous international awards. "No agency in this part of the world has ever won a Cannes Gold Lion," Ismaili notes.

The monument is eloquent in its simplicity. "I will always refer to Leonardo da Vinci's quote: 'Simplicity is the ultimate sophistication,' and I really really believe in that," explains Ismaili. Newborn appears in almost every shot taken in Prishtina, the capital of Kosovo, by local or international reporters. It appeared on the front page of *The New York Times* and many other newspapers and publications around the world. The unveiling ceremony was live on CNN, BBC, and other major networks. Kosovo, to this day is referred as "the newborn country" by many media outlets.

RIGHT
Ogilvy created a website for Newborn addressing the facts about the
project, and posted movies of the
celebration on YouTube. There are
photos and live video coverage from
Kosovo national television on the
Newborn Facebook page, which has
over 15,000 fans. The sculpture has
both a physical and virtual monument to the idea of freedom.

How to Do a Design Critique

Nearly all designers were trained in giving and receiving design critiques while in art school. It is the most common form of feedback, and is generally done in a public group scenario. Designers may want to explain to their clients how to critique the design solutions in order to get the most value and useful information possible. In a critique, designers need to uncover their client's true opinions about the design solution they are presented with. It is important to avoid discussion of what exactly the designer needs to do to make something better. Rather, a critique should generate information that the designer reviews, then incorporates into the next phase of work on the design.

Here are the key steps and questions to consider in a design critique:

Overview

→ Initial reactions: What is your first impression of the design?

→ Content: Is everything that should be included in the design there?

→ Aesthetics: Taken as a whole, what is the total overall effect? Does it feel right?

→ Style: Does the design seem appropriate for the stated goal or purpose?

2 → **Analysis**
→ Layout: Does everything seem to be in the right place?
→ Flow: Does the content appear in a natural and logical progression?
→ Usability: Is it easy to use or interact with the design?
→ Typography: Does the type feel appropriate in tone?
→ Color: How is color being used? What affect does it have in terms of conveying the desired message?
→ Missing: Is anything missing? Conversely, is anything there that shouldn't be?

3 → **Interpretation**
→ Audience: How do you think the target audience will respond to this design? Why?
→ Details: Is the use of these particular graphic elements consistent with the goals of this design? Why? Why not?
→ Problem areas: What things in this design are not as effective as they could be? Why?
→ Appeal: Is this an effective and appealing design for the context it will live in? Why? Why not?

4 → **Evaluation**
→ Brief: Does this design fulfill on the creative brief. If not, why?
→ Judgment: Given the answers to the above, does this design work?

Case Study Aesthetic Considerations

Stanley Wong / Hong Kong, China

Stanley Wong Ping-pui, also known as "anothermountainman," is an award-winning, Hong Kong–based advertising guru, graphic designer, photographer, filmmaker, and fine artist. He has held creative director positions at some of the world's largest advertising agencies in Asia, including J. Walter Thompson; Bartle Bogle Hegarty; and TBWA Hong Kong. "I was never taught how to draw—I just did it," says Wong. "In school, I was always assigned to do the school posters. I liked to enter logo design competitions, too. If I hadn't joined the graphic design and advertising field, I might have become a teacher. I was trained to 'teach' design, not actually 'do' it." Wong creates installations, both art projects and commercial environments, along with graphic design, branding, and television commercials. "I define myself as a social worker using visual communication as a tool to raise people's awareness on various issues."

Redwhiteandblue

Redwhiteandblue is an ongoing art, design, and social commentary project by Wong. This series, which takes the form of posters, installations, objects, and books, plays off of the ubiquitous red, white, and blue tricolor woven bags found in Hong Kong—the city's de facto flag. It conveys the positive spirit of Hong Kong using the colors as a jumping off point. The project won critical acclaim, and is part of the permanent collections at Hong Kong and Victoria & Albert museums.

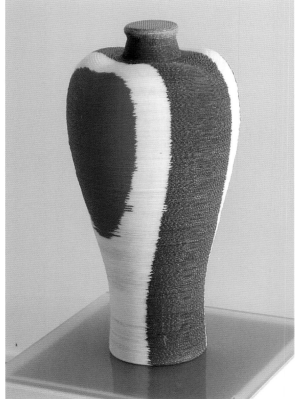

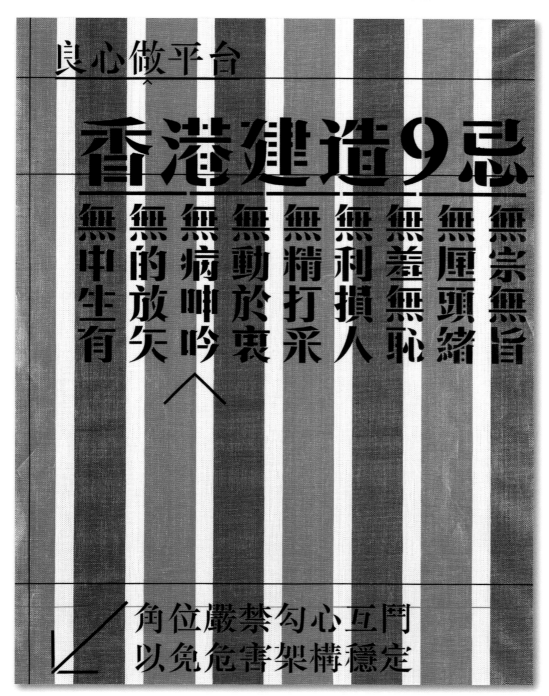

良心做平台

香港建造9忌

無中生有　無的放矢　無病呻吟　無動於衷　無精打采　無利損人　無羞無恥　無厘頭緒　無宗無旨

角位嚴禁勾心互鬥
以免危害架構穩定

The Redwhiteandblue posters, left, are silkscreened on colored fabric. Wong further explores the concept by creating fabric-wrapped three-dimensional objects, like the vases and jars, opposite. With this work, Wong uses a simple color scheme as a graphic unifier—both literal and symbolic. "Our Hong Kong, our home, since the '97 handover [to China], has become shrouded in an atmosphere of mutual distrust, noncommunication, and non-consensus," explains Wong. "I try to promote the positive spirit of Hong Kong in two and three dimensions."

Case Study Aesthetic Considerations

Stanley Wong / Hong Kong, China

Redwhiteandblue

The synthetic tricolor fabric was Japanese in origin, and produced in Taiwan for use as shopping bags. It has been in use since Hong Kong's British-ruled colonial days. Initially, this red, white, and blue cloth was used to make a popular bag for carrying foodstuffs and necessities from Hong Kong to mainland China through Shenzhen, the first city you reach after crossing the British/Chinese border. The fabric is still used as carrying bags, store canopies, coverings in construction sites, and other uses.

In high art and daily life, the fabric has become a kind of flag, symbolically acknowledging and reminding people of their Chinese heritage.

Wong transforms this ordinary stuff into something extraordinary to become an icon of Hong Kong and its people. He has created Redwhiteandblue for over a decade. Wong's intention is to tap into aesthetic preferences of Hong Kong and design things that spark conversation and open a dialogue about the city and its culture.

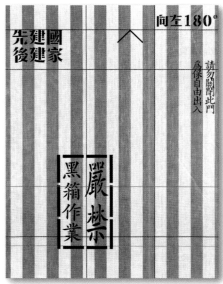

The LEE Ka-sing Gallery in Toronto, Canada, wrote about the series: "Wong approaches this tangible material with great sensitivity, seeing beauty in it, finding meaning in the inexhaustible applications Redwhiteandblue offers in everyday life. The process of continual discovery of this 'urban icon' in different Asian cities makes him post the questions: When and where? An identity which becomes more and more difficult to define, and increasingly blurry in the shifting landscape of globalism."

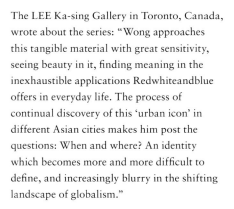

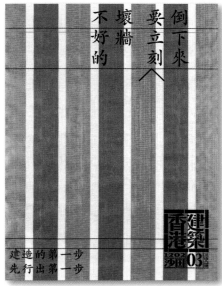

19°97-20°47

不移不變

三合三游 有十必有十 忌卜吞十游

Case Study Aesthetic Considerations

Stanley Wong / Hong Kong, China

The Cave Living of Exception / Act-itude

With an aim toward promoting Asian culture and beauty, the Exception / Act-itude retail environment, designed by Wong, features recycled or found objects to create a profound sense of passing time and the enlightened reuse of beautiful objects. It is a truly unique shopping experience. Located in Beijing, China, the store for this upscale retailer of ecofriendly clothing and home accessories for a sustainable lifestyle is divided into a variety of spaces. The shop features an art gallery, coffee corner, book corner, main fashion area, and fitting rooms. Rows of spotlights on beams are spread over the canvas ceiling, with smaller ceiling lights used to line the hay cave and floor spotlights that illuminate clothing displays and design features.

The Pawn

The Pawn restaurant and bar occupies one of the few old buildings left in the densely populated Wan Chai district of Hong Kong. Located on Johnston Road in a former site of the "Wedding Card Street," which is a casualty of recent urban renewal in the area. Whole blocks of buildings in this area have been razed and replaced. However, both Wong, who branded the Pawn and designed the interiors, and his client have an avid interest in Hong Kong history and its preservation. The restaurant building once housed a pawn shop, and the design nods to this aesthetic while being a very modern eating and drinking establishment. The food and atmosphere is that of a uniquely Hong Kong gourmet pub.

Getting Aesthetic Ideas Approved

A critical responsibility of a designer is selling the client on a design as it was concepted. Accomplishing this is part informing and part charming, with a whole lot of salesmanship thrown into the mix. A designer who can't, or won't, effectively win clients over will soon find themselves unable to get their best ideas approved. Some tips on persuading:

Set the tone
Be on time, dress to impress, show the client respect. Set the stage for them to receive the presentation and listen to you in a positive frame of mind.

Summarize the background
A previous meeting should have gone over the research and strategy for the work. Sum it up again so that the client truly understands the context. Reinforce that this design is not an arbitrary decision.

Tell them a story
Explain briefly how this concept works. Do it in narrative form. How the idea evolved from their goals and is a logical conclusion embodied in the aesthetics of this design.

Employ relevant buzzwords
Refer back to the client's own language from briefings. For example, if they wanted to "dominate" or "reignite," tell them that this design does exactly that.

Give them an aesthetic solution hook
Provide something clearly definable that is also memorable. Explain the concept as a sound bite that obviously solves their problem. Let this be the takeaway they can explain to others.

Know when enough is enough
Make your case. Do it with confidence. Then stop talking and invite feedback. Think before you speak, especially avoid defense mechanisms.

Project Profile in Aesthetic Considerations: Voice

More Singles, Couples and Queens **designed by Voice / Adelaide, Australia**

More Singles, Couples and Queens, Exhibition Catalog

Voice is an Australian multidisciplinary design consultancy that delivers solutions in digital media, environmental, identity, packaging, promotional, publications and typeface design. At the heart of their practice is a love of developing new ways of communicating with alluring and engaging visuals. The firm, lead by codirectors

Anthony De Leo and Scott Carslake, had worked with artist Toby Richardson in the past to develop the catalog for his series of photographs of old discarded mattresses. This second series (and exhibition), *More Singles, Couples and Queens*, continues documenting the strangely compelling portrait of people's lives as told through these once-loved, but now rejected, ordinary household items.

The photographs appear life-size in the exhibition, and the oversized design of the catalog was chosen to express that idea. "It needed to be large and clumsy like a mattress, and the size is proportionate to that of a single mattress," Carslake notes. We wanted the viewer to be able to see all the details as if you were actually holding a mattress. Having the fold-out pages and size ensured people wrestled with the catalog at exhibition opening. The artist loved this, it reminded him of when he had to physically collect each mattress from the trash himself."

More Singles, Couples and Queens, Exhibition Catalog

Meant as a companion, not a literal document of the exhibition, the catalog is sent to collectors, museums, galleries, and curators who may not have the opportunity to see original body of work. Therefore, it was critical the design makes a statement as well as communicating the artist's original intention to this wider audience. "The catalog is different from others as the artist's work allowed us to present it unexpectedly," explains Carslake. "We cropped into the qualities that made each mattress unique. The stitched binding and custom labels applied to the cover are representative of the tactile qualities of the subjects. The size and format of the catalog adds to the impact."

"*More Singles, Couples and Queens* challenges conventional notions of photographic portraiture," says the artist, Toby Richardson. "This work captures the remarkable individuality of each mattress, in their fabric design, age, and history; some stunningly decorative; others rich with color; some stained; each unique; they are metaphoric portraits of their previous owners." The catalog invites the reader in to bring out the intricate qualities of each mattress. "It was also very important for the catalog to encourage the viewer to look beyond mattresses as an object to see the beauty in the fabric, and in the same breath be challenged at what might be a urine or blood stain," says Anthony De Leo. The catalog has helped the artist attract international attention, resulting in numerous exhibitions and inclusion in important art publications.

Managing by Voice

Voice has some very specific and useful methods of managing client relationships. Here are three key points:

1. Communication must be clear, open, honest, and respectful

- It is vital that clients understand what you are proposing, discussing, and advising.
- Honesty is essential in our opinions and advice, as well as information about fees, fee variations, and contract agreements.
- We are respectful of our clients' time, personality etc.
- It's important to be pleasant and understanding.

2. Explain concepts effectively

- We always ask clients to remove themselves from the project and disconnect their emotions when we present concepts. This is extremely difficult for them, but we need them to put themselves in the position of their audience.
- Presentations are as close to the real thing as possible, so what clients see is almost exactly like what they will be getting. Our experience is that a high percentage of clients cannot accurately imagine an idea if they are not seeing the physical concept; this can introduce confusion and lack of confidence.
- Present ideas and concepts a client cannot refuse because the process and results are taking them to new exciting places—beyond their expectations.

3. Partnering with clients and forming enjoyable relationships

- We view our clients as design partners—we need them in order to get the right result.
- Clients enjoy being involved in the process because it creates a strong rapport.
- If they enjoy our personalities and we deliver tangible results, they will return in confidence and relationships grow and develop.

Chapter 8
Managing Expectations

How to Manage Client Expectations

Great design takes great designer and client collaboration. As we've seen in the preceding pages, there are many facets to the design process that must be managed. This book has focused on concept development:

▶ How design works to solve problems
▶ How design has been used to tackle society's goals while serving client businesses
▶ How research informs design; how strategic thinking is developed
▶ Why taking calculated risks makes design more effective
▶ How aesthetics plays a huge part in the success of a design
▶ How all of this must be contained in a creative brief
That is a lot to accomplish, and yet, every design project requires these things be done. All of these activities must be managed by the designer and the client, working together in partnership to achieve great results.

Client Interactions Mean Expectations

One of the most critical aspects of creating a great design is managing the client expectations. What is an expectation in the context of graphic design? Essentially, it is the belief that something will happen or be achieved. It's that simple, and that complex. Why? Because sometimes a client's true expectation is never fully expressed until it goes unmet. Then and only then, does the designer get the full insight into their client's true desires. However, meeting all of these client expectations, spoken or not, is an essential component of customer satisfaction. That means addressing what client's expect and how they interact with the designer throughout the concept development process. A universal and very reasonable client expectation is that the designer will fulfill on the assignment as outlined in the creative brief to the best of their ability, and complete the work on time and on budget.

Clients need to clearly understand what is occurring at each stage of the design process. They need to know when they are expected to contribute information, content, feedback, or even design fees. Clients also need to be prepared to review designs and must be made to understand what design can and cannot do. It doesn't serve the designer, but most importantly, the client themselves, if the client harbors unreasonable expectations. For example, a new website will not save a client's badly run or unstable business. It can help present the client as seemingly stable and well run, but it is up to the client to actually accomplish that.

Unexpressed
Expectations

Client Satisfaction
(Great Design)

Exist in the
Creative Brief

Exist Only in
Clients Mind

Client Satisfaction

There are a lot of details and variables in the early phases of the design process. Complete client satisfaction should always be the goal, after all, a happy client is a repeat customer, so it pays to keep them happy. Here are some things a designer must do to help insure just that:

- Understand their client's communication style and speak to them in a way they prefer.
- Clarify the design process including what a client needs to do and when they need to do it.
- Encourage client feedback at appropriate times in the development process, and respond to it—either by doing what they suggest, or not doing it, but convincing the client that that is okay.
- Corral the client into a specific number of revisions at specific, logical points in the process. Avoid unnecessary and costly scope creep, i.e., expansion of the assignment beyond what has been contracted.
- Avoid unnecessary confrontations. Essentially, pick your battles with a client, but know when to graciously admit defeat and move on without holding a grudge.

Here are some things a designer should avoid:

- Working without an agreement on the nature of the project, the timeline, and the exact scope of work. All of these things should be included in the designer–client contract.
- Misusing a creative brief—either not developing one in the first place, or not referring to it if one has been created.
- Poor communication with the client. Put detailed process information, requests or revisions, and client feedback in writing. Also, don't agree to do something in a verbal discussion, and then neglect to inform the design team about that conversation.

- Annoying the client by not acknowledging their requests, whatever they are. Better to be upfront and let them know that you cannot or will not fulfill their requests.
- Drama of any sort, which is usually based on personality clashes or anger due to unmet needs. Keep things professional.
- Selling out. This can take several forms, like a designer caving into a client's request even though they know it doesn't ultimately serve their client's goals. Another classic is going against a designer's own convictions and doing work they don't like for people they can't stand. Better to just get a new client and project. Just walk away in as timely and professional a manner as possible.

Meeting client expectations is a dance—a well choreographed set of intricate maneuvers. Designers can get quite good at it. One of the best things they can do is to listen, listen, listen to the client and respond immediately. Nip problems in the bud, and stop things from going from bad to worse.

What about unexpressed expectations? The only thing a designer can do is try to ferret them out. The best way is to spend time with their client. Talk about the client's business and their project extensively. Go through all the steps and activities outlined in the book and participate in them wholeheartedly, and get the client to do the same.

ABOVE
Managing client expectations to create 100 percent satisfaction means a designer must determine the expressed and unexpressed beliefs, needs, and desires that the client has for the design. Only when these are fulfilled is the client happy and the design process can be considered a successful collaboration.

Project Profile in Managing Expectations

Saraswat Bank designed by Umbrella Design / Mumbai, India

Saraswat Bank

Mumbai-based Umbrella Design was engaged to rebrand and reposition India's oldest and largest cooperative (privately held) bank. The goal was to transition the ninety-two-year-old Saraswat Bank to meet the needs and expectations not only of the bank's current stakeholders but also attract new, often younger, banking customers. Umbrella Design had to carefully lead their ultraconservative client through a thorough explanation of the branding process, so they created a

PowerPoint presentation. "We decided that our presentation would have to educate the audience about design and the advantages of good design, how design can keep a brand relevant and command a premium," explains Deven Sansare, creative director of Umbrella Design. "Then we went on to define the bank's problem, identify the opportunity, how we arrived at the brand emotion, and finally, present the design options. We had 40 minutes and 300 slides."

BELOW
Unlike most banks in the world, this bank was not created to make money, but to offer "help" to its own community members, the Indian ethnic group, the Saraswats. This guiding principle needed to be leveraged and also expanded upon.

Umbrella Design wanted to reaffirm that the bank's original personality could be maintained as it evolved. The designers identified a central brand emotion—"a sense of belonging." All the stakeholders shared this belief.

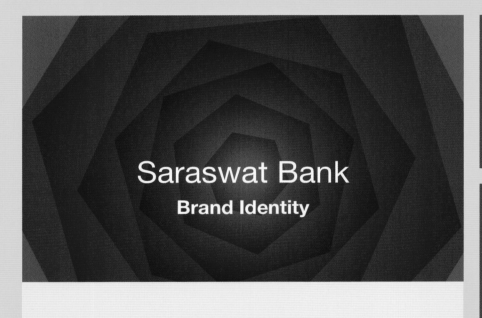

Saraswat Bank
Brand Identity

But when is change necessary for a brand?

To reflect a new or changed reality of a brand.

The environment has changed as well. Today, a bank is not an institution any more. **It is a Retail Brand.**

BELOW
There was equity in the bank's
ninety-year-old logo. Umbrella
Design did a variety of identity
explorations, some an adaptation,
others using a fresh approach. A
hexagon, chosen for its symbolic
reference to infinite connectivity
became a central containing shape
for the logo.

BELOW
The new logo was mocked up
in a variety of real-world applications, from stationery to bank
environments, in order to place the
identity in contexts that the bank's
stakeholders could understand
and visualize. The design was
very well received.

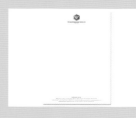

4 Best Practices for Successfully Managing Client Expectations

1. Identify and define the expectation.
If you've done a creative brief, you've essentially completed this. The exercise of doing the brief clearly defines specific details and measurable goals. (See Chapter 6 for more information.)

2. Educate and empathize with the client.
If you don't inform your client about how the work will proceed and what exactly they will see and need to do throughout the process, then you will have failed to educate them on how to be a designer's client. When you listen carefully to a client and read between the lines as well, you will come to empathize with your client. You'll also be getting inside your client's world-view and unspoken expectations. Do this as early as possible in order to make the design process run more smoothly.

3. Continuously check in and monitor the client.

Double-check on how each phase of the design process has affected your client. Were there any unspoken reactions? Second thoughts? Any additional information or insights? Also monitor the workflow. Is everything going as promised? Is the design process on time and on budget?

4. Influencing and persuading the client.

As they say, perception is reality. A designer can't change or influence a client's perception about a design, or their own working relationship, unless the client trusts them. As we all know, trust must be earned and that takes time. Salesmanship in design is often about persuading, and here again, trust is central to its effectiveness.

Project Profile in Managing Expectations:

CNN Grill designed by Collins: / New York, New York USA

CNN Grill

Collins: is an innovative, brand building agency lead by chairman and chief creative officer, Brian Collins. The New York–based agency specializes in communications, experiences, products, digital interactions and environments that transform the relationships between organizations, brands, and people. All of this expertise is spotlighted in their work for CNN Grill created as part of the 2008 American presidential election process. Within a matter of a few weeks,

a fortress-like building located across from the Democratic National Convention Hall was created to became a public forum for political discussion. Collins: along with CNN and Civic Entertainment Group worked together to make a unique gathering space. Long hours spent working or attending the political convention made the CNN Grill common ground for journalists, delegates, political operatives, celebrities, and ordinary citizens to relax after long sessions.

BELOW
The assignment was to translate CNN's brand platform into a meaningful, direct experience at the CNN Grill. In a democracy, politics are inclusive to everyone, so visitors were asked: "What does politics mean to you?" This sense of participation was enhanced further by a video wall that featured images of visitors taken as they entered the space. Google lists over a million links to reports that were filed from the CNN Grill, most by ordinary citizens, using CNN's iReport tools at free computer stations. Anyone at the grill could tell the nation what was going on, and they did. Eloquent and profound, the voices of ordinary Americans become the touchstones for the CNN Grill design.

T-shirts were popular with visitors (right). "Nothing fancy" is the design aesthetic. Even the custom-brewed ale looks down-home, (far right). Like the weathered signage outside, the Collins: team designed the label and the taps to feel like they had always been there (below).

CNN Grill

"Nothing fancy" was the design aesthetic chosen for the CNN Grill. Even the custom-brewed ale looked down-home. Like the weathered signage outside, the Collins: team designed the label and the taps to feel like they'd always been there. "We wanted the CNN Grill to look like it had been there a while," says Brian Collins. "The bottom detail shows how the team achieved the weathered look of Denver's old 'ghost' signs. The goal was to make the building familiar and surprising at the same time."

BELOW
The wisdom of citizens transforms the old warehouse building. Each line of type is an individual declaration. Instead of a fortress, the building becomes an icon of democratic thought. "CNN = Politics" was more than a slogan; it became a fact at the CNN Grill.

Communication and Design Management

Clients expect designers to be creative. That's a given. However, what some designers fail to recognize is that client's also want their designers to be confident and manage their projects well. The confidence comes through when a designer makes good creative choices and presents them well—they explain what it means, why the design is appropriate, and why it will work to meet the client's stated objective. This confidence also shows up in the way the designer speaks about the work and handles client questions. There is an air of sureness and leadership that allows the client to trust the designer's professional opinion. Client doubts about a design, or a designer's ability and expertise for that matter, can undermine any project. So by all means, be confident about the work you present to a client.

Clients don't typically ask a designer questions like
- What are your management skills like?
- How well do you organize and execute your work?
- What will it be like to collaborate together to get this project off the ground and in front of the audience?

If clients understood how much design management, not just creativity, was essential to successful design, they would probably spend a lot more time reviewing a designer's qualifications and abilities in this area as well.

Recognizing Design Management

Most clients look at a designer's portfolio, and if they see a project that is similar in nature and scope, especially for a big name client, they assume that the designer has the chops to handle a project of this nature well. However, a portfolio review never tells the design management story. Not really. A lot of assumptions get made. It would be in both the designer's and the client's best interest to discuss process and management style at length, relating the discussion to the projects in the portfolio, not just talking about the appearance of the work. It would also be a good idea for a design firm that is considering hiring a new designer, especially at a senior level, to have this type of discussion before any hiring decisions are made. Getting inside and understanding how a designer works and manages the process is so important.

What Good Communication Means

A huge part of design management is communication. Not just an easy and professional rapport, good communication in the design process also means
- Setting up jobs properly via a contract
- Providing progress reports and meeting notes
- Informing and/or persuading in a series of email exchanges throughout the project
- Developing a creative brief and design criteria documents
- Proper billing

It's a good idea to get things in writing that can serve as a kind of insurance policy in the event of a design project or client relationship turning sour. A collection of documents that proves that the client did indeed request certain things or agree to other things can be evidence of client knowledge, participation, and approval of the design process.

Ongoing Design Management

This book has dealt with the early phases of the design process. Here are some things a designer faces in the next phases of work:

- Project management
- Organizing project details
- Planning and budgeting
- Assembling an appropriate design team
- Managing creative people as well as clients
- Ensuring profitability

If you remember that it all boils down to thorough and effective communication, you're on the right path to managing the design process really well.

Directory of Contributors

AdamsMorioka
Beverly Hills, CA / New York, NY USA
www.adamsmorioka.com

Brand New School
New York, NY / Los Angeles, CA USA
www.brandnewschool.com

Culture AD
Atlanta, GA USA
www.culture-ad.com

Alexander Isley, Inc.
Redding, CT USA
www.alexanderisley.com

Change is good
Paris, France
www.changeisgood.fr

Fibonacci Design Group
Los Angeles, CA USA
www.fibonaccidesigngroup.com

ALT GROUP
Auckland, New Zealand
www.altgroup.net

Chase Design Group
Los Angeles, CA USA
www.chasedesigngroup.com

Finn Creative
Kununurra, Australia
www.finncreative.com.au

Asylum Creative Pte Ltd
Singapore
www.theasylum.com.sg

Citizen Scholar, Inc.
Brooklyn, NY USA
www.citizenscholar.com

Good Design Company
Tokyo, Japan
www.gooddesigncompany.com

Aufuldish & Warinner
San Anselmo, CA USA
www.aufwar.com

Collins:
New York, NY USA
www.collins1.com

Iconologic
Atlanta, GA USA
www.iconologic.com

Imaginary Forces
Los Angeles, CA / New York, NY USA
www.imaginaryforces.com

Paprika
Montreal, Canada
www.paparika.com

Umbrella Design
Mumbai, India
www.umbrelladesign.in

Jessica Hische
Brooklyn, NY USA
www.jhische.com

Saatchi & Saatchi Russia
Moscow, Russia
www.saatchi.ru/e

VOICE
Adelaide, Australia
www.voicedesign.net

Marco Morisini Studio
Pesaro, Italy
www.marcomorosini.com

SamataMason
Dundee, IL USA / Vancouver, BC, Canada
www.samtatmason.com

Weiden + Kennedy Tokyo
Tokyo, Japan
www.wk.com

Modern Dog
Seattle, Washington, USA
www.moderndog.com

smashLAB Inc.
Vancouver, BC, Canada
www.smashlab.com

Willoughby Design
Kansas City, MO USA
www.willoughbydesign.com

Ogilvy Albania + Kosovo
Tirana, Republic of Albania / Pristina,
Kosovo
www.ogilvyal.com

Stanley Wong
Hong Kong, China
www.threetwoone.com.hk

Index

A

Adams, Sean, 128
AdamsMorioka, Inc., 108–109, 156–161
aesthetic strategy, 94–95
aesthetics, 154–187
  case studies in, 166–171, 178–183
  components of, 163
  defined, 154
  dynamics, 164
  evaluation of, 172–173
  getting approval for, 184
  key questions about, 165
  mapping, 164
  project profiles in, 156–161, 174–175, 185–187
  truths about, 162
  universals, 155
African Pride, 62–63
Alexander Isley, Inc., 136–141
Alt Group, 15–17
Annenberg Community Beach House, 156–161
applied creativity, 14–25
Ascent, 46
Asylum, 118–123
audience
  defining the, 72–75
  media choice and, 76
  understanding the, 51, 70
Aufuldish, Bob, 144–145
Aufuldish & Warinner, 144–145

B

Beauty 360, 30–32
Benjamin Bixby, 19
Bennis, Warren, 7
blended research, 61
Borealis, 47
bottom line, 50–51
brand equity, 29
Brand New School (BNS), 126–131
branding, 52–57
Brimm, Craig, 62, 64
budget, 9
businesses, design requirements of, 14

C

case studies
  Asylum, 118–123
  Brand New School (BNS), 126–131
  Chase Design Group, 30–35
  Culture Advertising Design, 62–65
  Finn Creative, 86–93
  Good Design Company, 98–103
  Imaginary Forces, 52–57
  Modern Dog Design Company, 166–171
  smashLAB, 44–49
  Stanley Wong, 178–183
  in strategic thinking, 86–93
  Weiden+Kennedy, 38–41
CEO leadership, 124
Change Is Good, 25, 116
Chase Design Group, 30–35
Chocolate Research Facility, 122–123
Citizen Scholar, Inc., 67–69
classic design research, 61
client satisfaction, 191
clients
  building trust with, 50
  compatibility between designers and, 24
  design workflows and, 21
  expectations of, 18, 190–199
  feedback from, 173
  getting approval from, 172, 184
  importance of design to, 17
  managing relationships with, 187
  working with, 14
CNN Grill, 196–198
collaborative workflow, 21
College Sustainability Report Card, 48–49
Collins:, 196–198
communication, 9
  design management and, 199
  internal, 36–37
competition, 18
concept ideas, 10, 11, 20
Corban, Ben, 15

creative briefs, 134–151
  creation of, 135
  defined, 134
  vs. design criteria, 146
  going without, 148
  important things to include in, 142–143
  managing to, 146
  project profiles in, 136–141, 144–145, 149–151
  as strategic tools, 134
  users of, 147
creativity, applied, 14–25
Creme of Nature Professional, 65
culture, 72
Culture Advertising Design, 62–65
Currency magazine, 116
Cusp Conference, 82–83
customer intimacy, 81
CVS/pharmacy, 30–32

D

Danish Design Centre (DDC), 17, 50
de Brito, Sam, 92
decision making styles, 124
delivery media, 9, 76–77
demographics, 61, 72
design
  act of, 14
  aesthetics in, 154–155
  competitive advantage from good, 6
  getting approval for, 172, 184
  impact of, 6–7
  importance of to clients, 17
  as innovation, 17
  measuring, 50–51
  power of, 18
  as process, 17
  role of, in achieving big goals, 28–57
  socially responsible, 42–49
  as strategic business tool, 84
  as styling, 17
  touchpoints, 28
  value of, 14
Design Can Change, 44–45

design concepts, preliminary, 10
Design Council, 50, 57
design criteria, 146
design critiques, 176–177
design idea flow, 21
design leadership, 6–7
design management
  communication and, 199
  defined, 6–7
  time spent on, 14
Design Management Institute, 50
design process
  factors affecting, 9
  as iterative process, 20
  steps in, 10–11
design process chart, 9–11
design research, 60–77
  case study in, 62–65
  defining the audience, 72–75
  design thinking and, 70
  scale and focus of, 66
  tactics, 71
Design Research Society, 70
design strategy, 80–111
  aesthetic strategy, 94–95
  articulation of, 107
  common mistakes in, 110
  defined, 81
  development of, 85
  elements of, 84
  evaluation of, 106
  project profiles in, 82–83, 96–97, 104–105, 108–111
design teams, 21
design thinking, 29, 70
designers
  choosing, 24
  compatibility between clients and, 24
  work process for, 20–21
designism movement, 28
development phase, 11
differentiation, 80
DJ Uppercut, 39
Duessing, Ryan, 67
Dutton, Denis, 155

E

Elizabeth Arden Red Door Spas, 136–141
Emirates Airlines, 126–127
employee communications, 36–37
environmental media, 77
ethnography, 61, 72–73
Exception / Act-itude, 182
expectation management, 190–199
experience, 72
experience design, 52–57
experiental branding, 52–57
exploration phase, 10

F

Fainting Goat, 166
feedback, 173
Fibonacci Design Group, 37
Finn Creative, 86–93
focus groups, 61
Form Gallery, 89–91
Full Throttle, 33

G

Ganesha campaign, 22–23
Gehlhaar, Jens, 130
Gelganyem Trust, 88, 89
global issues, 28–29
globalization, 38–41
Good Design Company, 98–103
Google, 38
graphic design. see design
ground zero redesign, 56–57

H

HGM Branding, 15–17
Hische, Jessica, 43
Hudson Gavin Martin (HGM), 15–17
Hunt, Randy J., 67–69

I

Iconologic, 19
ideas
  development of, 10–11, 20
  flow of design, 21

identity, 72
Imaginary Forces, 52–57
informed risk taking, 114–131
innovation, 17, 20, 31, 124
internal communications, 36–37
interviews, 71
ITOKI, 102

J

Japanese Graphic Design
Association (JAGDA), 99
Jemapur, 41

K

K2 Japan, 167
Karjaluoto, Eric, 44, 45
Kukuyo Design Awards, 100

L

Laforet Harajuku, 103
leaders, traits of, 7
Leccia Catalog, 25
Lee, Chris, 118
Les Allusifs, 96–97
Levonelle, 131
Little Village, 120
Logan Collection Vail, 144–145

M

managers, traits of, 7
manufacture/launch phase, 11
Marco Morosini Studio, 111
market research, 61
medium, defining, 76–77
Mister Nut, 111
Mizuno, Manabu, 98, 101, 102,
103
Modern Dog Design Company,
166–171
*More Singles, Couples and
Queens* Exhibition Catalog,
185–187
multitasking, 18
Museum of Modern Art
(MoMA), 53

N

Newborn Monument, 174–175
Nickelodeon Magazine, 43
Nike, 40
Nisbet, Todd, 55
nondesign, 17
Norman, Donald A., 162
Northern British Columbia
Tourism, 48
Notaro, Jonathan, 126, 127, 131

O

observational research, 61, 71
OfficeMax, 127
Ogilvy Albania & Kosovo,
174–175
Olay Total Effects, 104–105
Olive, 168–171
on-air media, 77
online media, 77
operational excellence, 81
orientation/research phase, 10
Ortega, Kenny, 55

P

Paprika, 96–97
participation, 61
The Pawn, 183
personas, 61
Phinney Neighborhood
Association (PNA), 168
photo ethnology, 61
Poole, Dean, 15, 16
Porter, Michael, 80
Potsunen project, 98
power, of design, 18
print media, 77
produce leadership, 81
product life cycles, 18
production phase, 11
project completion, 11
project initiation, 10
project profiles
    in aesthetics, 156–161, 174–
    175, 185–187
    in applied creativity, 15–19,
    22–23, 25
    in big goals, 37, 43
    in creative briefs, 136–141,
    144–145, 149–151

in design-centric research,
67–69
in expectation management,
192–193, 196–198
in informed risk taking, 116
in strategic thinking, 82–83,
96–97, 104–105, 108–111
project workflow, 9–11
prototype testing, 61
psychographics, 61, 74–75

R

Raye, Robynne, 166, 167
Readers Make Leaders, 64
Redwhiteandblue, 178–181
refinement phase, 11
research
    blended, 61
    case study in, 62–65
    design, 60–77
    ethnographic, 61, 72–73
    failure, 70
    market, 61
    methods, 60–61, 66, 71
    psychographic, 74–75
    scale and focus of, 66
    user experience, 61
research phase, 10
revisions, 51
Rhamnathkar, Bhupal, 22
risk/risk taking, 114–131
    assessment of, 115
    case studies in, 118–123,
    126–131
    encouragement of, 114
    innovative design and, 124
    presenting risky ideas, 125
    project profiles in, 116
    vs. uncertainty, 117
Rollins, Matt, 19

S

Saatchi & Saatchi, 104–105
SamataMason, 82–83
Sansare, Deven, 192
Saraswat Bank, 192–193
schedules, 9
scope of work, 9
SEI (Sustainable Endowments
Institute), 48–49

Sharwood's, 128
Shelkie, Eric, 44
smashLAB, 44–49
socially responsible design, 42–49
solo workflow, 21
Soy Joy, 130
SPIN! Neapolitan Pizza, 149–151
Starbucks, 34–35
Steiner, George, 80
Strassburger, Michael, 166
strategic thinking
    case studies in, 86–93, 98–103
    project profiles in, 82–83, 96–97, 104–105, 108–111
strategy, 80–81, 84, 94–95. *see also* design strategy
strategy phase, 10
Sun Microsystems, 37
Suntory, 99
Supermarket, 67–69
surveys, 71
sustainability, 29, 43–49

T

Times of India, 22–23
Times of Jakarta, 118–119
timing, 9
Tokyo Midtown, 101
triple bottom line, 50–51
trust building, 50

U

UCLA Anderson School of Management, 108–109
Umbrella Design, 22–23, 192–193
uncertainty, 117
United Architects, 56
Urban Intelligence, 64
user experience research, 61
Utter Rubbish, 121

V

VALS (Values and Lifestyles), 74–75
value disciplines, 81
value shifts, 29
van Gastel, Mikon, 56

Victoria's Secret Fashion Show, 54
visual anthropology, 61
Voice, 185–187

W

W+K Tokyo Lab, 39, 41
Web analytics, 61
Weiden+Kennedy, 38–41
Willoughby Design, 149–151
Wizard of Oz, 90

Wong, Stanley, 178–183
workflow, 21
Wunan, 86–87
Wynn Las Vegas, 55

Z

Zappos, 129

Bibliography

For Further Reading (books/pamphlets)

AIGA, *An Ethnography Primer*, AIGA in collaboration with Cheskin (2008).

Steven Pinker, "The Blank Slate: The Modern Denial of Human Nature, Penguin (2003).

George Steiner, *Strategic Planning*, Free Press (1979).

Michael Treacy and Fred Wiersema, *The Discipline of Market Leaders*, Addison-Wesley (1997).

Kenichi Ohmae, *The Borderless World*, McKinsey & Company, Inc., (1991).

W. Chan Kim and Renée Mauborgue, *Blue Ocean Strategy*, Harvard Business School Press (1995).

Brenda Laurel and Peter Lunenfeld, *Design Research*, Massachusetts Institute of Technology (2005).

Thomas Lockwood & Thomas Walton, *Building Design Strategy: Using Design to Achieve Key Business Objectives*, Allworth Press (2008).

Sicco van Gelder, *Global Brand Strategy: Unlocking Brand Potential Across Countries, Cultures & Markets*, Kogan Page Ltd. (2003).

Tad Crawford, *AIGA Professional Practices in Graphic Design*, Allworth Press (1998).

Clement Mok, *Designing Business: Multiple Media, Multiple Disciplines*, Adobe Press (2005).

Tom Peters, *The Professional Service Firm50*, Alfred A. Knopf, Inc. (1999).

Cameron Foote, *The Creative Business Guide to Running a Graphic Design Business*, Cameron S. Foote (2009).

Denis Dutton, "The Art Instinct: Beauty, Pleasure, and Human Evolution," Bloomsbury Press (2009).

For Further Reading (articles)

Michael Porter, "What is Strategy?," *Harvard Business Review* (November–December 1996).

Janet Rae-Dupree, "Design Is More Than Packaging," *The New York Times*, (2008).

Tim Brown, "Strategy By Design," *Fast Company* (2007).

Rob Wallace, "Design ROI Re-envisioned." *STEP-inside-design* (2007).

David Stairs, "Why Design Won't Save the World," *The Design Observer Group* (2007).

Pat Matson Knapp, "Position Design as a Strategic Business Element," *HOW*, (2008).

Resources

Design Organizations

AIGA (American Institute of Graphic Arts)
www.aiga.org

AIGA Center for Practice Management
http://cpm.aiga.org/

Association of Product Management and Product Marketing (AIPMM)
http://www.aipmm.com/

Association of Professional Design Firms (APDF)
https://www.apdf.org/

D&AD
http://www.dandad.org/

Danish Design Council
http://www.ddc.dk/

Design Can Change
www.designcanchange.org

Design Institute of Australia
www.dia.org.au

Design Management Institute
www.dmi.org

Design Research Society
www.designresearchsociety.org

JAGDA (Japanese Graphic Design Association)
www.jagda.org

The Association of Registered Graphic Designers of Ontario (RGD Ontario)
www.rgdontario.org

Design Council UK
www.designcouncil.org.uk

Acknowledgments

Thank you to the many contributors to this book. Thanks also to Emily Potts, Winnie Prentiss, Betsy Gammons, David Martinell, Cora Hawks, and the entire Rockport team. My heartfelt gratitude goes to Sean Adams, Noreen Morioka, and all of AdamsMorioka—a lovely job. A tip of the hat goes out to my many colleagues who have shared information, especially through AIGA. The influential business of graphic design thinkers who have influenced me: David Goodman, Ed Gold, Roger Whitehouse, Emily Ruth Cohen, Shel Perkins, David Baker, Maria Piscopo, Tad Crawford, and Cameron Foote. Much of what is covered in this book was learned via trial and error. Thanks to all the designers and clients I have worked for and with over the years for the opportunity to make mistakes, and finally, get it right, some times. Thank you one and all.

About the Author

Terry Lee Stone is a design management consultant and writer based in Los Angeles. She has worked with AdamsMorioka, The Designory, and Margo Chase Design, among others. Her clients have included: BMW Group DesignworksUSA, Adobe Systems, American Express, USC, and the Sundance Film Festival. Stone has taught the business of design at CalArts, Art Center College of Design, and Otis College of Art and Design. She is co-author of The Logo Design Workbook, and the author of *The Color Design Workbook*, a second AdamsMorioka book. She has written for several design magazines, including *STEP Magazine, Dynamic Graphics Magazine* and *AIGA Voice*. Terry was on the Board of Directors of the AIGA in Atlanta, Los Angeles, and Miami where she also served as the chapter's president. She has presented lectures and workshops for numerous organizations, such as AIGA and the Art Directors Club of New York.